How Do I Get to HEAVEN?

How Do I *Get to* HEAVEN?

TRAVELING THE ROMANS ROAD

Pamela L. McQuade

ISBN 978-1-61626-209-9

Published by Barbour Publishing, Inc., P.O. Box 719, Uhrichsville, Ohio 44683, www.barbourbooks.com

Our mission is to publish and distribute inspirational products offering exceptional value and biblical encouragement to the masses.

Printed in the United States of America.

CONTENTS

INTRODUCTION
What Is the Romans Road?

The Romans Road is a name given to the following seven verses in the book of Romans that describe the essentials of coming to faith in Jesus Christ. These verses have been helpful to people who want to know what they must do to become a Christian and to those who want to share their faith in Jesus.

> *As it is written: "There is no one righteous, not even one."*
>
> Romans 3:10 NIV

> *For all have sinned and fall short of the glory of God.*
>
> Romans 3:23 NIV

> *Therefore, just as sin entered the world through one man, and death through sin, and in this way death came to all people, because all sinned.*
>
> Romans 5:12 NIV

For the wages of sin is death, but the gift of God is eternal life in Christ Jesus our Lord.

ROMANS 6:23 NIV

But God demonstrates his own love for us in this: While we were still sinners, Christ died for us.

ROMANS 5:8 NIV

If you declare with your mouth, "Jesus is Lord," and believe in your heart that God raised him from the dead, you will be saved. For it is with your heart that you believe and are justified, and it is with your mouth that you profess your faith and are saved.

ROMANS 10:9–10 NIV

For, "Everyone who calls on the name of the Lord will be saved."

ROMANS 10:13 NIV

The Jewish apostle Paul wrote the book of Romans to the highly cosmopolitan church in the Roman Empire's capital city. Rome was home to about a million people, some from foreign lands, including a fair number of Jews. In many ways, Rome was like our cities today. In its prosperous environment, the well-to-do elite lived for today and their immediate pleasures, while a sizable portion of Rome's population slogged out their lives in tenements, existing in a state of perpetual hardship and danger in seedy neighborhoods. Numerous slaves or recently emancipated slaves made up a good portion of the population. Religion in Rome was a mixed bag; worship of pagan gods and cults of various sorts flourished in the numerous temples, while other people sought an understanding of an often-chaotic world by looking to magic for answers. Many of the more well-to-do Romans, including some of the emperors, gave themselves over to the desires of the flesh.

Paul had not yet founded the Roman church. In fact, when he wrote his letter to the Romans, he had yet to visit there. But he had heard much of their faith and prayed for them, asking that he might be sent to visit them (see Romans 1:8–9). Around AD 57 he wrote to this church, which was doubtless a mixture of some Jews and many Gentiles.

The letter Paul wrote to the Christians at Rome is his most heavily theological writing. In it the apostle explains much about how mankind comes to know God and how believers can better live a practical Christian life. Those who read his words received a good grounding in the theology of Christianity and valuable information on how to live as believers.

The information Paul gave to the early church is as helpful today as it was back then. Paul helps every reader understand what it means to be a Christian and how believers can effectively share their faith. The apostle knew how to build a church by training its people in the important elements of the faith, and we can also make good use of his methods and theology.

Those who have not yet come to belief in Jesus will find Paul's description of the faith sometimes daunting, often entrancing. To know Jesus is undoubtedly the best use anyone can make of life, and Paul encourages all who hear or read this message to come to know Him, too.

CHAPTER 1
A Terrible Dilemma

As it is written:
"There is no one righteous, not even one."
ROMANS 3:10 NIV

When a child is born, the family looks adoringly at the little baby, who appears to be just perfect, a wonderful new human being. Thinking about the future of this child, with all his hope and potential, the new parents are filled with excitement. They imagine the productive, happy life, filled with many blessings, which will be his. And in turn the child's parents feel blessed with a gift from God—a product of their own genes. A newborn child is a delightful creation who will walk down the road of life, learning new things and going wonderful places.

Everyone who is born into this world walks down a road of discovery. None of us know exactly where we are going or what will happen along the way. As we follow the road, we learn more about ourselves and the world around us. Sometimes life seems wonderful, and everything goes our way, but at other times we struggle. This isn't always an easy world to live in. We don't always do the right thing, and people aren't always nice to us.

Innocent or Perfect?

If these proud parents had to describe their newborn child, they would probably use the word *innocent*. After all, he has not had time to do anything wrong. And in part, they would be right. This young Adam has yet to even grab a favorite toy away from his sister or talk back to his parents. Yet even from the very beginning, this seemingly perfect baby is not as perfect as his family would like to think. Yes, he has ten tiny fingers and ten little toes. He has that wonderful, clean, new-baby smell. He is beautiful. But even in one so small there lies within the ability, even the willingness, to do wrong. Fail to give that baby his bottle, and you will soon hear his complaints. If his mother is busy filling another of his needs, he cannot think, *I won't complain, because I know she's doing something good for me.* In a moment, he will be screaming at the top of his lungs.

Though it may not seem fair to blame a baby for an instinct he is too young to control, the truth is still there. Baby Adam falls short of the person he was created to be, and he is so much less than the perfect nature of the God his parents hope he will one day accept as his Savior. Like every other human, he has been damaged by the sin Adam and Eve brought into the world. And if no one accepts that truth now, in a couple of years everyone will know it when he hits the "terrible twos." Truly, even innocent Baby Adam is unrighteous—he is not as perfect as the God who created him, so he cannot relate to Him perfectly.

The Beginning of the Problem

The first couple had been created without sin. God made each of them and placed them in a beautiful garden, filled with plants and animals.

> *So God created man in his own image, in the image of God he created him; male and female he created them.*
>
> *And God blessed them. And God said to them, "Be fruitful and multiply and fill the earth and subdue it and have dominion over the fish of the sea and over the birds of the heavens and over every living thing that moves on the earth." And God said, "Behold, I have given you every plant yielding seed that is on the face of all the earth, and every tree with seed in its fruit. You shall have them for food. And to every beast of the earth and to every bird of the heavens and to everything*

that creeps on the earth, everything that has the breath of life, I have given every green plant for food." And it was so. And God saw everything that he had made, and behold, it was very good. And there was evening and there was morning, the sixth day.

GENESIS 1:27–31 ESV

It must have been a wonderful existence in which this couple had a deep, satisfying relationship with their Creator. So where did the imperfection problem start? Eve and Adam got all humanity into trouble when they chose to disobey God's warning:

"You are free to eat from any tree in the garden; but you must not eat from the tree of the knowledge of good and evil, for when you eat from it you will certainly die."

GENESIS 2:16–17 NIV

God might as well have said to the couple, "Just do this one thing for Me, leave this tree alone." It wasn't a big thing—He wasn't asking them to go hungry, just to avoid that one tree. But because humans are what they are, it was like putting a plate of rich chocolate cake in front of a child and telling her not to eat it.

Instead of clinging to God's command, Eve

listened to Satan when he pointed out that eating this forbidden fruit would give her the ability to know good and evil. Though she didn't understand exactly what that meant, in one moment the fruit that hung from that one forbidden tree looked awfully good. Unaware of the trauma that knowledge would cause, Eve succumbed to curiosity and took a bite from the tempting fruit:

> *When the woman saw that the fruit of the tree was good for food and pleasing to the eye, and also desirable for gaining wisdom, she took some and ate it. She also gave some to her husband, who was with her, and he ate it.*
>
> Genesis 3:6 NIV

When the erring woman offered the fruit to her spouse, he didn't say no. Perhaps Adam wondered what it would be like to know good from evil. Would it give him more power? Greater abilities? Make him more like God? No matter what he thought, scripture doesn't record his balking at the idea of disobeying God.

Though this couple had known nothing but good from God, they chose to disobey His single command that limited their freedom. In that moment, they fell into unrighteousness—an act that would affect all of humanity.

What Is Righteousness?

Not surprisingly, *righteousness* isn't a word most of us—except pastors, theologians, and maybe a few serious Christians—use very often. Maybe we're even a bit fuzzy on what it means.

Though the Merriam-Webster dictionary defines *righteousness* as "acting in accord with divine or moral law: free from guilt or sin," in Christian terms, righteousness has more to do with the character of God than with some deed on our part. He is a holy God, and our actions cannot reflect His nature because sin has marred our entire beings. Though the dictionary editors might like to think this definition is spiritually accurate, it is overly optimistic because it implies we can be free from guilt or sin by trying to do the right thing.

In his *Expository Dictionary of New Testament Words*, W. E. Vine defines the Greek word for "righteousness," *dikaiosune*, as being:

> *"The character or quality of being right or just;" . . . It is used to denote an attribute of God, e.g., Rom. 3:5, the context of which shows that "the righteousness of God" means essentially the same as His faithfulness, or truthfulness, that which is consistent with His own nature and promises; Rom. 3:25,*

> *26 speaks of His "righteousness" as exhibited in the death of Christ, which is sufficient to show men that God is neither indifferent to sin nor regards it lightly. On the contrary, it demonstrates that quality of holiness in Him which must find expression in His condemnation of sin.*

What does it mean for God to be holy? His very nature is glorious, separated from every impurity. He is completely righteous and perfect, far beyond anything we could hope to become. He never fails or falls into sin. The comparison between our nature and His leaves us in the dust. We fail the righteous test, and only He is holy and worthy of worship (see Revelation 15:4).

How Much Righteousness Do I Need?

When God talks of righteousness, it's complete righteousness. So being mostly righteous isn't enough. We can't enter heaven by being 50.000001 percent righteous—even 99.999999 percent of righteousness wouldn't be enough. Either you are fully righteous or you aren't. That's why the popular idea of earning one's way into heaven is so preposterous. None of us can do well enough in the righteousness department to slide into heaven, because God can accept only those who are perfectly righteous. You either are worthy of heaven or you aren't. No one slides into heaven.

If we ask how much righteousness is enough, we're basically asking how much sin we can get away with. The answer is *none*. God is perfect, and we need to be, too. Even the smallest bit of sin is enough to separate us from Him. One wicked thought or criticism or one wrong act would prove how imperfect we are in comparison to the God who created us.

Scripture doesn't debate the truth of mankind's sin. It simply defines it by saying, "All wrongdoing is sin" (1 John 5:17 ESV). Then it takes away all our excuses by declaring, "Surely there is not a righteous man on earth who does good and never sins" (Ecclesiastes 7:20 ESV).

If we're honest with ourselves, we must admit that we—and all other humans—make mistakes and even intentionally do wrong. Some of us may do wrong less often than others, but compared to God we are all pitifully imperfect. His hallmark is 100 percent righteousness, and ours is sin. Like our ancestors, Adam and Eve, we cannot avoid this reality.

Even while the family of a newborn is making much of their new and beautiful addition, counting those fingers and toes over and over again, young Adam has been influenced by the sin of his ancestors. Before he has done one intentionally selfish act, because of his inheritance from that first couple, he is already set on a road that leads to physical and spiritual destruction. The Bible warns us, "The soul who sins shall die" (Ezekiel 18:4 ESV). That means both spiritual death and physical death are part of this life, and young Adam cannot avoid it any more than the rest of us can.

Hearing the Bad News

Naturally, none of us like to hear that we have sinned badly enough to deserve death. We would prefer to think we somehow escaped punishment. But God clearly tells us that even the best of us are hopelessly marred by sin. The apostle Paul describes this situation to his Roman audience by reviewing a number of Old Testament verses:

> *"There is no one righteous, not even one; there is no one who understands; there is no one who seeks God. All have turned away, they have together become worthless; there is no one who does good, not even one."*
>
> *"Their throats are open graves; their tongues practice deceit."*
>
> *"The poison of vipers is on their lips."*
>
> *"Their mouths are full of cursing and bitterness."*
>
> *"Their feet are swift to shed blood; ruin and misery mark their ways, and the way of peace they do not know."*
>
> ROMANS 3:10–17 NIV

Paul isn't picking on the Romans here; he's saying that no one has escaped sin's grasp. In the first two chapters of the Romans epistle, Paul considered the spiritual condition of the people of his own nation and that of the other Gentiles to whom he had brought the gospel:

> *The apostle reassumes his former assertion [in the previous chapters of Romans], and supports it, that a carnal circumcised Jew is no better than a carnal uncircumcised Gentile; it being already sufficiently made to appear, that they are both under the power and guilt of sin; and as a further evidence of it, he produces [in Romans 3:10–17] several passages out of the book of Psalms, and out of the prophecies of Isaiah, which fully express the sad corruption of human nature.*
>
> JOHN GILL

Take a look at the following verses, in slightly different translations, which make up Paul's review of the Old Testament truths in Romans 3:10–17.

> *The fool says in his heart, "There is no God." They are corrupt, doing abominable iniquity; there is none who does good. God looks down from heaven on the children of man to see if*

there are any who understand, who seek after God. They have all fallen away; together they have become corrupt; there is none who does good, not even one.

Psalm 53:1–3 esv

Not a word from their mouth can be trusted; their heart is filled with malice. Their throat is an open grave; with their tongues they tell lies.

Psalm 5:9 niv

They make their tongues as sharp as a serpent's; the poison of vipers is on their lips.

Psalm 140:3 niv

His mouth is full of lies and threats; trouble and evil are under his tongue.

Psalm 10:7 niv

Their feet rush into sin; they are swift to shed innocent blood. They pursue evil schemes; acts of violence mark their ways. The way of peace they do not know; there is no justice in their paths. They have turned them into crooked roads; no one who walks along them will know peace.

Isaiah 59:7–8 niv

This was grim news indeed for those who prided themselves on their own righteousness. All their hopes of being worthy of God clattered to the ground. Obviously Paul didn't come up with this idea of humanity's sinfulness on his own. The bad news about sin was already part of the Old Testament scriptures that the Jews had been familiar with for centuries. Sin has grieved both God and humanity for a long time—from those ancient days up to the present time.

Starting Down the Romans Road

In declaring our inability to be righteous, Paul has started us on what has been called the Romans Road. This consists of seven passages from the book of Romans that describe the plight of humanity in its sin and outline God's solution to the problem. All of us must begin our spiritual journey with the admission that no one but God is righteous.

Like every other human being, as young Adam embarks on his journey of discovery, he is faced with two roads. Eventually he will have to make a choice: Will he take the Romans Road or the way of sin? Will he admit that he, like every other human being, is steeped in sin and is not God's equal? Or will he declare that he is as good as any other human and turn away from God?

Bleak as God's condemnation of humanity is,

we have to admit it's true. None of us, under his or her own power, is the equal of God. No person has the moral quality of the One who never delights in wickedness, evildoers, or liars (see Psalm 5:4–6).

The New Testament describes sin with the word *hamartia*, which means to "miss the mark." Just look at the world around us, filled with people who take advantage of others, the pain of divorce, businesses filled with dishonesty, and a host of other ills. Can we honestly claim that sin has not damaged us—and our world? Who has not missed the mark of God's righteousness?

> *God has a high and holy standard of what is right, and so long as man follows the divine standard he will see himself as he truly exists in God's eyes. The flat statement of the Almighty is that all men have fallen far short of God's required standard. . . . God has established His standard of perfection for entry into heaven, and all men have "missed the mark" as an archer's bow would fall to the ground because it fell short of its target.*
>
> Lehman Strauss

Though God gave us commandments to point the way toward Himself and promised that they would be our righteousness (see Deuteronomy

6:25), we have never followed those laws perfectly. The Old Testament includes the Ten Commandments, which establish man's responsibility to God and his fellow man. The first five books of the Old Testament also provide God's directions about the importance of holiness. Anyone who wants to understand what God the Father is like and how to please Him will find much information in these passages.

Yet even all this information has failed to change our minds and hearts. Even when we really want to please God, we often fall short. Why? Because sin entered our lives long before we were aware of it and remains persistent in its influence on us.

Matthew Henry describes the impact of sin, which remains a great burden for every individual, even those who only pretend to follow Christ:

> *All mankind are under the guilt of sin, as a burden; and under the government and dominion of sin, as enslaved to it, to work wickedness. This is made plain by several passages of scripture from the Old Testament, which describe the corrupt and depraved state of all men, till grace restrain or change them. Great as our advantages are, these texts describe multitudes who call themselves Christians. Their principles and conduct prove that there is no fear of God before their eyes. And where no fear of God is, no good is to be looked for.*

Relating to God

Not only does sin weigh us down, but as a result of it the prophet Isaiah describes the difficulty sinners have in relating to God:

> *You [Lord] come to the help of those who gladly do right, who remember your ways. But when we continued to sin against them, you were angry. How then can we be saved? All of us have become like one who is unclean, and all our righteous acts are like filthy rags; we all shrivel up like a leaf, and like the wind our sins sweep us away. No one calls on your name or strives to lay hold of you; for you have hidden your face from us and have given us over to our sins.*
>
> Isaiah 64:5–7 NIV

In short, God is holy and we aren't. His nature is perfect in every detail; goodness shines out of Him, and He is never unjust. As a holy God, He cannot ignore sin. His holy nature requires that He treat it with justice and cause the sinner to pay the price for his wrongdoing.

Imagine that you were brought up in a good home where everyone was honest and did the right thing. No one ever lied or stole or did anything that was even faintly wrong. Suddenly a crisis entered your life, and you were forced to live with a family that was just the opposite of yours. Everyone was constantly lying, stealing, and being thoroughly untrustworthy. If you had to live there for long, it would make you crazy, wouldn't it?

That's just a faint picture of what it would be like if our righteous, powerful God ignored sin. Worse than making Him crazy, it would go against everything He is. Sin simply cannot exist where the Lord is. The Bible describes His nature in these words: "'Who is like you among the gods, O LORD—glorious in holiness, awesome in splendor, performing great wonders?'" (Exodus 15:11 NLT). His holy nature totally opposes sin. And in His power, as ruler of all He has created, He cannot slip sin under the rug just because some sinners would like it that way.

Some people would like to turn the blame for their sin back on God. A "good" God, to their mind, would not make them suffer this way or punish them for their wrongdoing. They try to make God appear wicked, because there is suffering in the world. But in doing this, they don't solve the problem of pain; instead they deny the need for justice. They have created a god who serves their own desires, and they have turned away from the Lord who is so good that He cannot ignore sin because it causes pain.

In His wisdom, God uses suffering to draw many people to Himself. As His justice is served, so is mercy. He provides justice, through the sacrifice of His Son, who takes the place of sinners on the cross. Through this same act He also provides a gracious, compassionate, and merciful way for people to approach Him and begin a deep relationship of love with their Creator.

Understanding God's Holiness

How can we even begin to understand this holy being? Could we ever be in the least bit like Him? If we tried to be righteous, what would we aim for?

Because God wants us to know Him—in Jesus, the God-man sent to earth—He gives us a picture of what He is and the righteousness mankind was meant to demonstrate:

> *Righteousness as exemplified by Christ is not merely the absence of vice or the presence of virtue. It is a consuming passion for God which sends you forth in His name to establish His kingdom.*
>
> Irving Peake Johnson

To say that in our own nature, we find God impossible to know is to make light of the situation. Though God requires that people have a consuming passion for Him, because of sin, each of us has a passion to fulfill our own desires. In our purely human state, we probably don't think often about God. And even if we do, we end up being more puzzled and doubtful than anything. Searching for Him and discovering how He wants us to live doesn't usually cross our sin-filled minds. We live mostly in confusion when it comes to knowing who the Lord is and what He requires of us.

This is the chasm lying between God and man. The rocky depths below the cliff that lies at our feet could never be bridged by anything we can do. All the steel and concrete in the world cannot change our nature and reach to the other side. We are born separated from God, and in our own power there is nothing we can do about it.

We are not righteous on our own, and we face a terrible dilemma about how to relate to God. Yet there is hope, even for this tiny Baby Adam. The prophet Isaiah spoke for God when he promised, " 'Though your sins are like scarlet, they shall be as white as snow; though they are red as crimson, they shall be like wool' " (Isaiah 1:18 NIV).

This is not a last-minute decision on God's part. He had our salvation in mind from the beginning of our lives, even when we could not be aware of it. David the psalmist declared, "You brought me out of the womb; you made me trust in you, even at my mother's breast" (Psalm 22:9 NIV). God has always loved us and will not desert us in our hopeless situation as sinners.

CHAPTER 2
The Problem of Sin

For all have sinned and fall short of the glory of God.
ROMANS 3:23 NIV

Every human being is stuck in sin, like a truck that has veered off the road into a muddy ditch. We all have followed the usual human map for life, have run off the straight and narrow road, and now we are in the trap of sin up to our hubcaps, with no way of escape.

Not only do we fail at doing right without even having to try, we sinners also actively work against the fulfillment of God's plans for the world. From the time we are born, like our forebears Adam and Eve, we are firmly under the sway of God's enemy, Satan. It's not that most of us thoughtfully and intentionally align ourselves with His enemy, but we are completely oblivious to God's call on our lives, and we sin without even thinking about it. Therefore we cannot even begin to work with God to bring about the plans He has for His creation.

Though Satan controls young Adam's life, he may not be aware of it for a long time. Without much thinking about it, until he recognizes God's claim on his life, our modern Adam will go against all God designed him to be and everything He planned for him to do. Young Adam will grow up and eventually be confronted by the truth that he cannot be righteous through his own efforts. When he recognizes that his sin has separated him from God, he will be standing on the second step of the Romans Road: "For all have sinned and fall short of the glory of God" (Romans 3:23 NIV).

At reading these words, Adam may feel tempted to despair. But he need not throw in the towel. Though his situation is desperate, he need not be, because God did not end the scriptures with those words, condemning him and the rest of humanity to an eternity without Him.

In Romans 3:20 (ESV), Paul says, "By works of the law no human being will be justified in his sight, since through the law comes knowledge of sin." In this verse, he describes the inability of human effort or God's law (the truths God gave His people in the Old Testament) to make people right with God. Knowing about sin is not enough; just identifying sin does not stop a person from committing it.

Paul follows this up by outlining another way to righteousness—the route God intended all along:

But now God has shown us a way to be made right with him without keeping the requirements of the law, as was promised in the writings of Moses and the prophets long ago. We are made right with God by placing our faith in Jesus Christ. And this is true for everyone who believes, no matter who we are.

For everyone has sinned; we all fall short of God's glorious standard. Yet God, with undeserved kindness, declares that we are righteous. He did this through Christ Jesus when he freed us from the penalty for our sins. For God presented Jesus as the sacrifice for sin. People are made right with God when they believe that Jesus sacrificed his life, shedding his blood. This sacrifice shows that God was being fair when he held back and did not punish those who sinned in times past, for he was looking ahead and including them in what he would do in this present time. God did this to demonstrate his righteousness, for he himself is fair and just, and he declares sinners to be right in his sight when they believe in Jesus.

Romans 3:21–26 NLT

Notice that our second step on the Romans Road is part of God's bigger picture of sin and redemption. Romans 3:21–22 shows that our own efforts will not gain us access to God. Romans 3:23 helps us recognize our profound need for Jesus.

Immediately after identifying the failure of sinners, the above passage of scripture speaks of those same people being justified, or made right with God, by faith. God has not left humans stuck up to their hubcaps in sin with no way out. He gives humanity a gift—His Son Jesus, who was crucified to buy unrighteous people back out of their sin.

From the time of Adam and Eve, all humans have made a personal bargain with Satan, selling themselves into sin by taking part in it. Though God created us, we have all sold ourselves into slavery to Satan in return for the short-term joys of sin. But our Creator has not left us in slavery. He sent Jesus to buy us back. We have been redeemed by His sacrifice on the cross. He was free of sin, but He chose to die in our place.

Those who accept this sacrifice, believing in Him as the One who died for their sins, will have their sins passed over and will have a lifelong relationship with God. The Bible has a word for this: *justification.*

Justification is an act of God's grace wherein He pardons all our sins and accepts us as righteous in His sight only for the righteousness of Christ

imputed to us and received by faith alone.
Westminster Shorter Catechism

Yet as we begin to rejoice in what God has done for us, we need to beware. While He offers us redemption from sin because we have faith in His Son, that does not give us an easy believism—"just say the right words and you will be saved." Though God provided a way for us to reconnect with Him, He does not lessen the importance of a real commitment to Him and a lifestyle that accepts His grace, leaves sin behind, and seeks to please Him. Taking Jesus as Savior is not a quick fix for a minor sin problem, but a lifelong obligation and service to God.

Taking Sin Seriously

God provides a rather simple way for us to have a deep relationship with Him. But we cannot enter into faith without understanding the gravity of our situation if we do not have Jesus as our Savior. Before we take any step, we need to know why we need a Savior and what we are being saved from.

First we need to recognize that we have sinned. But what is sin?

Sin is mankind's willful choice, in spite of the unceasing mercies and kindness of God, to refuse to honor Him by reflecting His character. God made us for that supreme purpose, but we determined to go the way of our own selfish preoccupations. Any action that does not reflect the character of the Creator in its motive and consequences is sin. It is an assault on God's prerogative to spurn God's glory and act in our own self-interests.

JOHN HANNAH

That's exactly what Adam and Eve did, and it's what all humans have done ever since the first couple ate that fruit.

Matthew Henry describes our natural condition before God, when we don't know Jesus as Savior:

All are guilty, and therefore all have need of a righteousness wherein to appear before God. For all have sinned *(Rom. 3:23); all are sinners by nature, by practice, and* have come short of the glory of God—*have failed of that which is the chief end of man.* Come short, *as the archer comes short of the mark, as the runner comes short of the prize; so come short, as not only not to win, but to be great losers.*

We cannot take our situation as losers too lightly, because that would cause us to rely again on ourselves for salvation—as if we could ever achieve it in our own feeble strength. The truth is that no good work can make us acceptable to God. The prophet Isaiah described our feeble efforts to do so: "But we are all as an unclean thing, and all our righteousnesses are as filthy rags" (Isaiah 64:6 KJV).

How Do We Sin?

In the Old Testament, three Hebrew words describe sin:

> *Hata' appears most frequently. . . . It means to fall short of the divine standards. 'Avon, often rendered "iniquity" or "guilt," means to twist the divine standards or to deviate from them. Pesha', translated "transgression" or "rebellion," is human revolt against God's standards or his expressed will.*
>
> REVELL BIBLE DICTIONARY

The most general word for sin in the New Testament, *hamartia*, means to miss the mark. We do so when we fail to live according to God's standards. W. E. Vine comments that a related word, *hamartema*, "denotes an act of disobedience to divine law."

We can sin by unintentionally falling short of God's commands or by twisting, avoiding, or resisting them. Many more words in the Bible also describe sin, including "disobedience," "error," "fault," "iniquity," "lawlessness," "ungodliness," and "wrongdoing." Whatever way we find to sin, God has described it for us in His Word.

Whom Do We Sin Against?

Scripture tells us that our unbelief in God hurts us (see Proverbs 8:36) and describes various ways in which humans harm one another by their sinfulness. But David clarifies that transgression is really a wrong against God, even more than against the people who are impacted by our sin.

> *Against You, You only, have I sinned, and done this evil in Your sight—that You may be found just when You speak, and blameless when You judge.*
>
> PSALM 51:4 NKJV

Though David, the king of Israel, had slept with Bathsheba and then killed her husband, he eventually recognized that his sin was ultimately rebellion against His Lord. God, David declared, was justified in sending the prophet Nathan to condemn him about his sin, because his wrongdoing deserved punishment.

By declaring that it was really God against whom he sinned, David stripped away all the he-saids-she-saids of his adultery and took the blame squarely on his own shoulders. That's what we need to do, too—face the facts that we have offended God and need to admit this to Him. Accepting the truth that we have been totally destroyed, spiritually, by sin puts us face-to-face with Jesus, whose sacrifice can redeem us from sin. Knowing that we desperately need help turns us to the Savior who can provide it.

Actually, Matthew Henry's above description of our situation is rather kind. Scripture does not just call us losers; even worse, it describes those who have not accepted Christ as hopelessly dead in their sin, and it depicts their godless lifestyle in unflattering terms:

> *As for you, you were dead in your transgressions and sins, in which you used to live when you followed the ways of this world and of the ruler of the kingdom of the air, the spirit who is now at work in those who are disobedient. All of us also lived among them at one time, gratifying the cravings of our flesh and following its desires and thoughts. Like the rest, we were by nature deserving of wrath.*
>
> EPHESIANS 2:1–3 NIV

The life we live without Christ may appeal to our us in sinful humanity, but it shows a terrible sin problem. And since a holy God cannot ignore sin, we deserve His wrath as punishment for it.

> *The wrath of God is being revealed from heaven against all the godlessness and wickedness of people, who suppress the truth by their wickedness, since what may be known about God is plain to them, because God has made it plain to them. For since the creation of the world God's invisible qualities—his eternal power and divine nature—have been clearly seen, being understood from what has been made, so that people are without excuse.*
>
> ROMANS 1:18–20 NIV

> *"He who believes in the Son has everlasting life; and he who does not believe the Son shall not see life, but the wrath of God abides on him."*
>
> JOHN 3:36 NKJV

> *But for those who are self-seeking and who reject the truth and follow evil, there will be wrath and anger.*
>
> ROMANS 2:8 NIV

We may not see God punish every wrongdoer here on earth, but we can still trust Him implicitly. If He does not exact retribution in this life, God will certainly visit His wrath on sinners in eternity.

Dead and deserving of God's wrath because of sin—this is the starting place of Baby Adam as he lies in his mother's arms. Even before he can think of wrongdoing, he is trapped in the tendency for sin that Adam and Eve passed on to him. Scripture confirms it: "Surely I was sinful at birth, sinful from the time my mother conceived me" (Psalm 51:5 NIV).

Though we may rebel at the idea of a tiny child starting so early on the way of sin, if we are honest, this truth is hard to ignore. No person—except the God-man Jesus Christ—has ever avoided sin. As innocent as Baby Adam appears, it will not be long before he wants his own way in life and does much to see that he gets it. No one will have to train him in sin; he will fall into it all on his own.

If Baby Adam, who is at the start of the roadway of life, is stuck in sin like a truck mired up to its wheels, are not we who have already proven our own unrighteousness even more stuck? Yet some people will still object to this idea of the sinfulness of all humanity and declare themselves in no need of salvation. The Bible warns them, "If we say that we have no sin, we deceive ourselves, and the truth is not in us" (1 John 1:8 NKJV).

Can those who object to God's judgment ignore the evil of this world? Where does it come from, if not from people who do wrong? Though some people do more wrong than others, every human has a problem with sin. None of us completely avoid it.

Romans 3:23 both points out our sin and the huge shortfall of our ability to reconnect with the God who would redeem us. Humanity cannot find its way out of sin by creating methods of passing judgment on those who are sinners. Because we are so flawed by sin ourselves, we do not have the ability to make a proper judgment about the goodness of others:

> *You, therefore, have no excuse, you who pass judgment on someone else, for at whatever point you judge another, you are condemning yourself, because you who pass judgment do the same things. Now we know that God's judgment against those who do such things is based on truth. So when you, a mere human being, pass judgment on them and yet do the same things, do you think you will escape God's judgment?*
>
> Romans 2:1–3 niv

All our judgments become self-righteousness and bring condemnation down upon us. When we judge others, we get ourselves deeper into sin. Only

God can make a truly impartial judgment:

> *But because of your stubbornness and your unrepentant heart, you are storing up wrath against yourself for the day of God's wrath, when his righteous judgment will be revealed.*
>
> ROMANS 2:5 NIV

Our situation seems totally impossible. Who is this God whose glory we cannot attain? What does He require of us? And how can we ever begin to relate to Him?

God's Glory

The Bible repeatedly describes God by calling Him glorious. But what are we talking about when we speak of this glory that we fall so short of?

> *God is the only being in all of existence who can be said to possess inherent glory. We don't give it to Him; it is His by virtue of who He is. If no one ever gave God any praise, He would still be the glorious God that He is, because He was glorious before any beings were created to worship Him. . . . His glory is His being—simply the sum of what He is, regardless of what we do or do not do in recognition of it.*
>
> JOHN MACARTHUR

The Israelites got a glimpse of God's glory when He revealed the Ten Commandments to Moses on Mount Sinai. They saw something of what God was really like. Because God's glory is not a comforting thing for sinful humans, His power terrified His people.

> *Then the Lord said to Moses, "Come up to Me on the mountain and be there; and I will give you tablets of stone, and the law and commandments which I have written, that you may teach them." . . . Then Moses went up into the mountain, and a cloud covered the mountain.*
>
> *Now the glory of the Lord rested on Mount Sinai, and the cloud covered it six days. And on the seventh day He called to Moses out of the midst of the cloud. The sight of the glory of the Lord was like a consuming fire on the top of the mountain in the eyes of the children of Israel.*
>
> Exodus 24:12, 15–17 NKJV

The Israelites must have wondered, *What will this awesome God do to us?*

The biblical God is not the convenient, tame god many would like to have—a cosmic Santa who gives endlessly and demands little of His people.

The glorious Lord of scripture consumes people one way or another. Either they give their lives to Him and are consumed by His glorious nature and with the desire to do His will, or their sin causes them to be consumed by His wrath (see Deuteronomy 6:5; John 3:36).

Not even one of God's greatest prophets could experience all of God's glory. When Moses sought to know the Lord more deeply and asked to see His glory, the Lord agreed. Yet He still had to protect the prophet, since no person could experience the fullness of His glory:

> *Moses said, "Please show me your glory." And he said, "I will make all my goodness pass before you and will proclaim before you my name 'The Lord.' And I will be gracious to whom I will be gracious, and will show mercy on whom I will show mercy. But," he said, "you cannot see my face, for man shall not see me and live." And the Lord said, "Behold, there is a place by me where you shall stand on the rock, and while my glory passes by I will put you in a cleft of the rock, and I will cover you with my hand until I have passed by. Then I will take away my hand, and you shall see my back, but my face shall not be seen."*
>
> Exodus 33:18–25 ESV

God is awesome in His glory—a truth those Israelites recognized, but a reality most sinners fail to appreciate. *That* is the crux of the problem. Though God created a world that reflected Himself, humanity ignored and opposed Him. They never gave Him the place and worship that He rightly deserved. Then they tried to replace him with feeble pagan gods, made in the image of themselves and the animals He created. Not surprisingly, this caused mankind to experience His wrath:

> *The wrath of God is being revealed from heaven against all the godlessness and wickedness of people, who suppress the truth by their wickedness, since what may be known about God is plain to them, because God has made it plain to them. For since the creation of the world God's invisible qualities—his eternal power and divine nature—have been clearly seen, being understood from what has been made, so that people are without excuse.*
>
> *For although they knew God, they neither glorified him as God nor gave thanks to him, but their thinking became futile and their foolish hearts were darkened. Although they claimed to be wise, they became fools and exchanged the glory of the immortal God for images made to look like a mortal human*

being and birds and animals and reptiles.

ROMANS 1:18–23 NIV

The psalmist David gives us a picture of the kind of worship the Lord deserves when he calls on all heaven to glorify God:

Ascribe to the Lord, you heavenly beings, ascribe to the Lord glory and strength. Ascribe to the Lord the glory due his name; worship the Lord in the splendor of his holiness.

PSALM 29:1–2 NIV

In a messianic hymn that portrays Jesus as the supreme ruler who is to be worshipped, David speaks of Jesus' glory, picturing Him as a victor in battle. The temple gates open for Him.

Who is the King of glory? The Lord, strong and mighty; the Lord, invincible in battle. Open up, ancient gates! Open up, ancient doors, and let the King of glory enter. Who is the King of glory? The Lord of Heaven's Armies—he is the King of glory.

PSALM 24:8–10 NLT

No person is as glorious or powerful as God, and all of us have failed to recognize His awesome nature. It's as if there were an elephant in our homes, and we simply attempted to live around it. Left to our own devices, we would never recognize God at all.

The Lord would clearly be within His rights to object to such treatment and condemn everyone in the human race. He created people, made a beautiful world in which they and animals could live, and invited the humans to have a relationship with Him. Shortly thereafter, Adam and Eve rushed to have things their own way.

Maybe the first couple couldn't quite forget paradise during their lives, but the generations that followed them had never been in the garden of Eden. Idols quickly replaced the glorious Lord whom their forebears had known intimately. Everyone began to worship the pagan gods that were nothing like the Lord. The Old Testament portrays the continual failure of the nations of Israel and Judah. Even after God had shown himself to them, they lapsed into idolatry instead of worshipping the one, true God.

Since then, all humanity has fallen away from the acknowledgment of God's supremacy. Still the Lord has not condemned people on a group basis. Just as He calls each person individually to enter into relationship with Him, each bears the guilt of his own sin:

"Yet you say, 'Why should the son not bear the guilt of the father?' Because the son has done what is lawful and right, and has kept all My statutes and observed them, he shall surely live. The soul who sins shall die. The son shall not bear the guilt of the father, nor the father bear the guilt of the son. The righteousness of the righteous shall be upon himself, and the wickedness of the wicked shall be upon himself."

EZEKIEL 18:19–20 NKJV

God works one-on-one with every person. The sins of Adam and Eve do not totally cut us off from Him. Rather than leaving us hopelessly in our sin, He offers us His grace, or unmerited favor. He still calls every person on earth to come into fellowship with Him through faith in Jesus Christ, His Son (see Matthew 11:28).

CHAPTER 3
The Cause of Death

Therefore, just as sin entered the world through one man, and death through sin, and in this way death came to all people, because all sinned.
Romans 5:12 NIV

As Baby Adam lies in his crib, sleeping peacefully or crying his lungs out because he has a need that hasn't been met, it's unlikely anyone thinks about death. His is a new, promising life. Yet none of his family members are so naive as to believe that Adam will live forever. From the time of Adam and Eve, no person has. Just as God warned, eating from the tree of the knowledge of good and evil in the garden brought death to all people (see Genesis 2:17). From the day we draw our first breath, death is a part of life.

The root cause of death is sin. We're not alone in sin. That sin ditch we're stuck in is really a huge parking lot that everyone gets caught in. Stuck trucks abound, all mired up with no way out. Every effort to free them has been unsuccessful, because no human has the power to do it.

The rescuers have taken away their towropes, because nothing has been strong enough to move these heavy trucks out of the mire, and no one knows what else to do. The would-be rescuers are at the end of their ropes, physically and emotionally. No one can take on sin and win. And as long as sin rules this world, death is its end result.

Sin's Influence on Humanity

When Adam and Eve took those first bites from the fruit of the tree of knowledge of good and evil, they got all humanity, even Baby Adam, into a ton of trouble. Like so many decisions people make, this one didn't affect just them. They passed on that spiritual crookedness to all their children—and their children passed it on to their children, and on and on through the ages.

Scripture doesn't explain just how that bent for wrongdoing was transmitted, but it provides us with a few details about how it affected humanity:

> *When Adam sinned, sin entered the world. Adam's sin brought death, so death spread to everyone, for everyone sinned. Yes, people sinned even before the law was given. But it was not counted as sin because there was not*

yet any law to break. Still, everyone died—from the time of Adam to the time of Moses—even those who did not disobey an explicit commandment of God, as Adam did. Now Adam is a symbol, a representation of Christ, who was yet to come.

Romans 5:12–14 NLT

God's law had yet to be written down when Adam and Eve sinned. But the truth about God's sinless perfection and man's sin still existed between the time of Adam and Moses, the prophet through whom God gave His law. Who God was and what He required of people never changed. Though God didn't personally tell individuals what to avoid, as He had told Adam and Eve, His creation and the world of nature still made His attributes apparent to every human being, so God held them accountable for their sin:

God shows his anger from heaven against all sinful, wicked people who suppress the truth by their wickedness. They know the truth about God because he has made it obvious to them. For ever since the world was created, people have seen the earth and sky. Through everything God made, they can clearly see his invisible qualities—his eternal power and divine nature. So they have no excuse for not knowing God.

Yes, they knew God, but they wouldn't worship him as God or even give him thanks. And they began to think up foolish ideas of what God was like. As a result, their minds became dark and confused. Claiming to be wise, they instead became utter fools. And instead of worshiping the glorious, ever-living God, they worshiped idols made to look like mere people and birds and animals and reptiles.

Romans 1:18–23 NLT

Though all people sin, Adam became the symbol of the sinner because he brought sin into the world. Though Eve sinned, too, the Bible uses her husband as the picture of the first sinner and the one who passed sin down to his descendants. Through the very first humans whom God placed on the earth, the entire human race became tainted with sin.

Though that couple started the problem of sin, none of us can escape sin by claiming it wasn't our fault. No person since Adam and Eve has had a heart that so fully desired to do God's will that giving up anything looked like a great idea. When the rubber meets the road, we all prefer to do what we want, not what God commands. Deep down inside, we had rather be our own gods than admit that Jesus is Lord and that we should obey Him in all things.

Here is the human predicament: We were created to obey God, and life works best when we do, but we have set ourselves up as little idols instead of well-loved, obedient children.

That rebellion against God has shown itself throughout human history, spreading to infect the soul of every person. Sin takes over the minds and hearts of all of us, until it has filled every corner of the world and every part of life:

> *Furthermore, just as [ungodly people] did not think it worthwhile to retain the knowledge of God, so God gave them over to a depraved mind, so that they do what ought not to be done. They have become filled with every kind of wickedness, evil, greed and depravity. They are full of envy, murder, strife, deceit and malice. They are gossips, slanderers, God-haters, insolent, arrogant and boastful; they invent ways of doing evil; they disobey their parents; they have no understanding, no fidelity, no love, no mercy.*
>
> ROMANS 1:28–31 NIV

Many people try to escape this truth. They want to believe they are fine just as they are. They cling to the ideas that they never do any serious wrong and that their good deeds can somehow get them into heaven. Like small children, they close their eyes and cover their ears to try to avoid the truth. Sin has destroyed our lives by separating us from God and damaging our relationships with other people. All society shows it, but these escapists go on believing there is nothing wrong. Though stuck in mud to the top of their hubcaps, they don't even realize it. They are living stuck inside their trucks when they could be traveling homeward on the highway.

The fact is that sin has destroyed our world. It didn't simply affect one group of people or influence people for a certain number of years. No one escapes the impact of sin on society, in the home, or in individual lives. The only way we can avoid facing the truth about sin is to pretend that God and sin do not exist. Many people have done that for a long time. But closing our eyes to sin cannot wipe it out. Avoiding thinking about it will not change anything. And most of all, it will not keep us from the end result of sin—death.

Death's Connection to Sin

The book of Romans is not the only place in the Bible where sin and death are linked. The book of Proverbs also sums up God's view of the subject: "He who sins against me wrongs his own soul; all those who hate me love death" (Proverbs 8:36 NKJV). No one ends up being unscathed when sin enters the picture.

This sin-death connection began in the earliest pages of Genesis, when the first couple faced the choice of whether to listen to God or Satan:

> *And the Lord God commanded the man, saying, "You may surely eat of every tree of the garden, but of the tree of the knowledge of good and evil you shall not eat, for in the day that you eat of it you shall surely die."*
>
> GENESIS 2:16–17 ESV

> *But the serpent said to the woman, "You will not surely die. For God knows that when you eat of it your eyes will be opened, and you will be like God, knowing good and evil." So when the woman saw that the tree was good for food, and that it was a delight to the eyes, and that the tree was to be desired to make one wise, she took of its fruit and ate, and she also gave some to her husband who was with her, and he ate.*
>
> GENESIS 3:4–6 ESV

Eve chose to listen to Satan, not God. It's not hard for us to understand why she made this choice. How unappealing the idea of death was in comparison to the beautiful tree, with its delightful fruit. Could anything that looked so good actually cause death? It must have seemed impossible. But with that one bite, she must have soon realized that the serpent had lied to her. Even though the fruit was not physically poisonous, death immediately took hold of her soul.

At first, it might have seemed to Eve that Satan was right. She didn't fall down and die as soon as she ate the fruit; neither did Adam when he tasted it. But something significant had changed in their lives. No longer did they value God the way they once had—a change that began when they chose not to believe Him instead of His enemy.

Just as we often try to avoid a person with whom we have had a disagreement, Eve and her husband no longer waited to commune with God. Instead, they hid from Him:

> *And they heard the sound of the Lord God walking in the garden in the cool of the day, and the man and his wife hid themselves from the presence of the Lord God among the trees of the garden. But the Lord God called to the man and said to him, "Where are you?" And he said, "I heard the sound of you in the garden, and I was afraid, because I was naked, and I hid myself." He said, "Who told*

> *you that you were naked? Have you eaten of the tree of which I commanded you not to eat?" The man said, "The woman whom you gave to be with me, she gave me fruit of the tree, and I ate." Then the Lord God said to the woman, "What is this that you have done?" The woman said, "The serpent deceived me, and I ate."*
>
> GENESIS 3:8–13 ESV

Adam and Eve could not hide their sin from God. Adam immediately tried to distract God's attention by telling Him they were naked. But once God pointed out they had eaten the forbidden fruit, the couple didn't admit their wrongdoing and take responsibility for it. For the first time, they used the tactic of evasion. Adam blamed his action on Eve. Then Eve blamed the whole thing on the serpent. The harm of disobedience had been done; their trusting relationship with God was history.

Not only that, but now that their relationship with God was shattered, all their other relationships were affected. Scripture doesn't tell us what the two said to each other afterward, but chances are good that Eve said, "Why did you blame me, Adam? After all, you didn't say no to eating that fruit." You can bet that Adam had a sharp reply in return.

God's Response to Sin

Of course, even before God confronted the couple, He had seen Adam and Eve's sin. He confronted them so they would understand the meaning of their disobedience, not because He just wanted to take them to task. John Gill describes this encounter following the fall of man, Christ's role in the situation, and the hope God offered as soon as the wrong had been done:

> *And they heard the voice of the Lord God . . .which they had heard before, and knew, though perhaps now in another tone, and very terrible, which before was mild and gentle, pleasant and delightful. . .the voice of the Son of God, the eternal Word, is here meant, who appeared in an human form, as a pledge of His future incarnation, and that not only as a Judge, to arraign, examine, and condemn the parties concerned in this act of disobedience to God, but as a Savior of men, to whom, as such, He made Himself known, as the event shows, and therefore they had no reason to entertain such terrible apprehensions of Him, as to flee from Him.*
>
> John Gill

The couple's actions, when they ate the forbidden fruit, clearly implied they believed God had lied to them, but He did not turn His back on them.

As judge, God had every right to punish His creation, and so He did. Eve would experience more pain in childbearing, and she would desire her husband, who would henceforth rule over her (see Genesis 3:16). Instead of having a blessed relationship with the land, Adam would have to struggle to provide for his family, scratching out a living from the ground by fighting off weeds. Now he would put a lot of hard work into making a living. Life became much harder as the couple learned to live without God's continual blessings (see Genesis 3:17–19).

But God's description of the hardships they would face was not the worst thing they experienced. Now they would have to leave their home in the idyllic garden and venture into the larger world. This removal was for their own safety, but it must have been a bitter thing as they left all they were familiar with and the Lord whom they had once relied on.

> *Then the Lord God said, "Behold, the man has become like one of us in knowing good and evil. Now, lest he reach out his hand and take also of the tree of life and eat, and live forever"—therefore the Lord God sent him out*

> *from the garden of Eden to work the ground from which he was taken. He drove out the man, and at the east of the garden of Eden he placed the cherubim and a flaming sword that turned every way to guard the way to the tree of life.*
>
> Genesis 3:22–24 ESV

But as hard as the separation between God and man was for Adam and Eve, it must have been even harder on God. For the Lord didn't simply call it quits on His relationship with His creation. He made provision to end this distance between Himself and man by offering forgiveness. As the offended party, He took responsibility for healing the broken relationship.

Is There a Solution?

So what exactly is the solution to this sin problem? Paul says in Romans 3:20 that even the works of the law do not solve it. And the apostle knew what he was talking about. Before he became a believer, Paul spent many years trying to do all the good he could to earn his way into God's favor. Where did his efforts lead to? Paul had a lively career as a Pharisee who persecuted Christians but still did not understand what the law required of him. Though he studied God's law and tried to live a rigorously moral life, salvation escaped young Saul (as he was then called).

Even after he was preaching the gospel throughout the world, the apostle admitted his own limitations when it came to sin:

> *I don't really understand myself, for I want to do what is right, but I don't do it. Instead, I do what I hate. But if I know that what I am doing is wrong, this shows that I agree that the law is good.*
>
> Romans 7:15–16 NLT

Though the law describes our problem and makes us aware of our own failings, it still cannot provide the solution to sin. The law says: "And if we are careful to obey all this law before the Lord our God, as he has commanded us, that will be our righteousness" (Deuteronomy 6:25 NIV). But we still have a problem. The law must be kept perfectly to guarantee our righteousness, and none of us can do that. So even by keeping the law, we cannot earn our way into heaven.

God's Word can awaken us to our own unrighteousness and point us in the direction we need to go. But even if we accept those truths, we have not been made right with God. It takes more than that—a personal response of faith: "For in [the gospel] the righteousness of God is revealed from faith for faith, as it is written, 'The righteous shall live by faith'" (Romans 1:17 ESV). Righteousness is impossible without the exercise of faith.

The Bible describes one man whose faith brought him righteousness: "What does Scripture say? 'Abraham believed God, and it was credited to him as righteousness'" (Romans 4:3 NIV). Abraham waited many years for the son whom God had promised him. Through this child, the nation of Israel would be born. As the years passed and no child appeared, Abraham did not lose faith:

> *Yet he [Abraham] did not waver through unbelief regarding the promise of God, but was strengthened in his faith and gave glory to God, being fully persuaded that God had power to do what he had promised. This is why "it was credited to him as righteousness." The words "it was credited to him" were written not for him alone, but also for us, to whom God will credit righteousness—for us who believe in him who raised Jesus our Lord from the dead. He was delivered over to death for our sins and was raised to life for our justification.*
>
> ROMANS 4:20–25 NIV

Abraham's faith was shown by his obedience to God when he waited for the birth of his promised son, then was willing to offer his son Isaac as a sacrifice (see Genesis 22:1–18). He showed his commitment to the Lord in whom he believed. But God did not end the crediting of faith with Abraham. It is the way He plans to save every person who will trust in Him.

The Righteousness Solution

Faith is the solution to the problems of sin and unrighteousness. "But people are counted as righteous, not because of their work, but because of their faith in God who forgives sinners" (Romans 4:5 NLT). To many people this might sound so ephemeral that it hardly bears consideration. But those who think like this do not have a clear understanding of faith.

Faith is what you really believe in, deep down in your soul. All your actions in life are determined by what you believe, because your whole worldview is affected by your beliefs.

You don't have to say a word to others for them to know what you really believe in. They will realize it by your actions. You've seen this in others, too. If a politician tells you he cares for his constituency but votes for bills that take advantage of them and line his own pockets, you know what he believes in—his own greed. If a pastor tells you he loves his congregation and takes a pay cut because many in his church are unemployed and can't put much in the offering plate, you know he's been honest with you—he is living sacrificially, as an example of his faith.

Every person has faith in something. The politician who lines his own pockets has faith in money, not God. Others have faith in material things that can't be taken into eternity. But in the end, those who trust in things of this world will find themselves entering eternity with empty pockets.

But we don't have to end our lives in despair. We aren't doomed to an eternity apart from God. Because all along He had a master plan that would nullify death's influence and give us the gift of life instead.

CHAPTER 4
Wages or Gift?

For the wages of sin is death, but the gift of God is eternal life in Christ Jesus our Lord.
ROMANS 6:23 NIV

The bad news that we have covered in the previous chapters is that sin has a price—death. We have learned the truth of that firsthand. Thomas Watson's statement, "Sin has the devil for its father, shame for its companion, and death for its wages," has been proved in our own lives. We know we have earned all of that with our lifestyle of rebellion against God.

But the good news is that the Lord isn't a bad-news God. He never planned on completely destroying all humanity, though He had to punish sin. From the very beginning, our Lord had in mind to make a gift of salvation to humanity, through His Son, Jesus. That's the Good News He wants to share with us.

God's Incredible Plan

We no longer have to sit up to our hubcaps in mud, without a way out of the ditch. That's because God sent help from outside our dilemma—powerful help that draws us out of the muck and sets us on a new road—one we don't even have a map for. If we accept His help, we are in for a whole new driving experience in a new truck—but more than that, we become new people with a new goal.

If we accept His gift, we no longer hold the wheel. God will control our way and bring us to a new end of the road—not a ditch along the side of the highway where we landed before, but a heavenly destination. There is a new map that guides us to a heavenly destination, and He will take us every mile of the way in safety.

From the very beginning, God had a plan to save His people from their sin, through one who would overcome Satan. Long before Jesus was born in Bethlehem, the book of Job commented on our situation and foresaw Him as the mediator between God and man, the One who saves the wretched sinner from the results of his own wrongdoing:

> *"Man is also chastened with pain on his bed, and with strong pain in many of his bones, so that his life abhors bread, and his soul*

succulent food. His flesh wastes away from sight, and his bones stick out which once were not seen. Yes, his soul draws near the Pit, and his life to the executioners. If there is a messenger for him, a mediator, one among a thousand, to show man His uprightness, then He is gracious to him, and says, 'Deliver him from going down to the Pit; I have found a ransom'; his flesh shall be young like a child's, he shall return to the days of his youth. He shall pray to God, and He will delight in him, he shall see His face with joy, for He restores to man His righteousness. Then he looks at men and says, 'I have sinned, and perverted what was right, and it did not profit me.' He will redeem his soul from going down to the Pit, and his life shall see the light."

Job 33:19–28 NKJV

This redemption that Job's friend Elihu spoke of became reality with the death and resurrection of Jesus. What Job could look forward to, trusting in faith, was shown clearly to all mankind many centuries after Job's time.

Yet Job recognized that this righteousness God gave to people was not something rooted in themselves: "I put on righteousness, and it clothed me; my justice was like a robe and a turban" (Job 29:14

NKJV). His description of being clothed in righteousness is a perfect picture of what happens. For the righteousness we have is not really our own. We still have within us the tendency to sin, and sometimes even powerful believers will fall mightily, as King David learned when he fell into sin with Bathsheba. Yet when we accept the fact that Jesus Christ died for our sins and take Him as our Savior, He covers our sins, and we receive His righteousness. David described it like this:

> *Blessed is he whose transgression is forgiven, whose sin is covered. Blessed is the man to whom the Lord does not impute iniquity, and in whose spirit there is no deceit.*
>
> PSALM 32:1–2 NKJV

We come to Jesus because He generously paid the price we could never have paid and draws us to Himself. If we accept His offer and are born again (see John 3:16) the Holy Spirit renews us, making it possible for us to live righteous lives. All of this came to us as a gift—there is no fee we have to pay to the rescuer, no hidden clauses in the agreement.

Paul compares God's gift to the unexpected and nasty "gift" of offense that came to Adam and Eve through Satan:

(But the free gift is not like the offense. For if by the one man's offense many died, much more the grace of God and the gift by the grace of the one Man, Jesus Christ, abounded to many. And the gift is not like that which came through the one who sinned. For the judgment which came from one offense resulted in condemnation, but the free gift which came from many offenses resulted in justification. For if by the one man's offense death reigned through the one, much more those who receive abundance of grace and of the gift of righteousness will reign in life through the One, Jesus Christ.)

Therefore, as through one man's offense judgment came to all men, resulting in condemnation, even so through one Man's righteous act the free gift came to all men, resulting in justification of life. For as by one man's disobedience many were made sinners, so also by one Man's obedience many will be made righteous.

Moreover the law entered that the offense might abound. But where sin abounded, grace abounded much more, so that as sin reigned in death, even so grace might reign through righteousness to eternal life through Jesus Christ our Lord.

Romans 5:15–21 NKJV

Like Adam's offense, Jesus' gift affected all humanity. But compare the scorecards of the offense that brought down all mankind and God's gift to humanity.

Adam's Fall
Price: death
One offense
Results in condemnation
Causes death to reign
Sin abounds

Jesus' Gift
Price: free
Came from many offenses
Gives eternal life
Causes many to reign in life
Grace abounds much more

The Fall limited all humanity, placing it in bondage to sin and giving death as its cost. But that's not the end of the story. Though Satan's wiles led the human race into sin, its influence still cannot overcome the plans of God. Satan's power to deceive cannot prevail over the cross, which is so much more powerful than Satan's delusion of mankind.

The sacrificial gift of Jesus' life—the death of one innocent person to ransom all those who were guilty—freed any who trust in Him to partake in eternal life. And He calls each one of us to accept this gift. It's not just for the important people or those who have certain spiritual advantages. It's for everyone: "Let the one who is thirsty come," His Spirit calls. "Let the one who desires take the water of life without price" (Revelation 22:17 ESV). All you need to be is thirsty for new life.

God's Gift of Grace

This way out of sin through Jesus' sacrifice came to us through God's grace—His favor given to us—though we did not deserve it. While we were trapped and stuck in our sin, Jesus came and rescued us. Though He didn't use a towrope or any other physical method, at the moment in which we trusted in Him to rescue us, He pulled us out of our mud-to-the-hubcaps trap and gave us a new lease on life:

> *God, being rich in mercy, because of the great love with which he loved us, even when we were dead in our trespasses, made us alive together with Christ—by grace you have been saved—and raised us up with him and seated us with him in the heavenly places in Christ Jesus, so that in the coming ages he might show the immeasurable riches of his grace in*

> *kindness toward us in Christ Jesus. For by grace you have been saved through faith. And this is not your own doing; it is the gift of God, not a result of works, so that no one may boast.*
>
> EPHESIANS 2:4–9 ESV

This change can be so sudden and so amazing, we might think there must be some catch. Don't we have to do something to be given this new life? But out of his free grace God completely opens our lives to the new world He has placed before us. We are made completely right with God—able to have an open relationship with Him in which there needs be no doubt or fear of punishment.

> *Grace does do this much: that we are accounted completely just before God. God's grace is not divided into bits and pieces. . .but grace takes us up completely into God's favor for the sake of Christ, our intercessor and mediator, so that the gifts may begin their work in us.*
>
> MARTIN LUTHER

This new life is no cheap or useless gift. It cost the Father the life of His only Son, a precious price indeed—for if a human life has value, how much more precious is the only One who is both God and man. There could be no greater value put on a person's life. The person who turns to God and values Him recognizes that there is nothing more costly in heaven or earth.

But what of those who reject this costly gift? God's grace is not a gift to be squandered on those who will not accept it. "When grace is shown to the wicked, they do not learn righteousness; even in a land of uprightness they go on doing evil and do not regard the majesty of the LORD" (Isaiah 26:10 NIV). Though all may hear the message, not everyone accepts this valuable gift. To those who refuse this gift, it seems a useless thing and anyone who trusts in it appears foolish.

Christians often have a hard time explaining to their unbelieving friends just why God is so wonderful and so real. It's like trying to explain a beautiful sunset to someone who has always been physically blind. How can you describe color and brilliance to a person who has no idea what they are? It's hard for that blind person to believe in something so beautiful.

In the same way, the tender relationship and freedom of real life that come with faith in Jesus are difficult to explain to someone who feels no need for freedom from sin. Some people will remain in that state, while God's Spirit will be able to lead others to take that necessary step of faith. Though God places salvation before all people, not everyone accepts the gift.

Despite human reluctance to trust in the invisible One, this is the very relationship humans were designed for.

> *What were we made for? To know God. What aim should we have in life? To know God. What is the eternal life that Jesus gives? To know God. What is the best thing in life? To know God. What in humans gives God most pleasure? Knowledge of Himself.*
>
> J. I. Packer

Knowing God is not a misery of limitations, as many non-Christians have imagined, but great delight. The psalmist describes the joys of life in God: "You make known to me the path of life; you will fill me with joy in your presence, with eternal pleasures at your right hand" (Psalm 16:11 NIV). But those who will not pleasure in Him will have none of those eternal pleasures. People must come to Him in faith in order to experience this particular type of joy.

This eternal joy is the life God had in mind for His people all along—not some pale and miserable existence, filled with sin, but a real, vivid eternal life, fulfilled through love for God.

What's Eternal Life Like?

So what is this new life that God offers? It not only bulges with spiritual joy and delight, but it affects every part of our existence.

> *It ought to be placed in the forefront of all Christian teaching that Christ's mission on earth was to give men life. "I am come," He said, "that ye might have life, and that ye might have it more abundantly." And that He meant literal life, literal spiritual and eternal life, is clear from the whole course of His teaching and acting.*
>
> Henry Drummond

Nor is it an unbelievable, off-in-the-future hope that impractical people cling to. Missionary Corrie ten Boom commented: "You know, eternal life does not start when you go to heaven. It starts the moment you reach out to Jesus. That is where it all begins!" Eternal life starts here on earth, in the lives of all believers.

What about Sin?

Well, you may be thinking, *if this eternal life is so wonderful and powerful, why aren't people living as if it were?*

Sin and temptation still affect Christians and will as long as they remain in this world. They still slip into wrongdoing and may not always provide a clear testimony to the truths they have experienced. But the big difference is that Christians are no longer bound by sin. Unlike those who have never known Jesus, they *can* say no to sin, even if they don't do so every time they are tempted.

Even though faithful believers face detours caused by doubt and sin, they begin to take hold of eternal life on earth and will certainly arrive safely at their final destination. After all, they are not depending on their own weak abilities to get them there, but on the God who promised, "Never will I leave you; never will I forsake you" (Hebrews 13:5 NIV). No matter how unfaithful Christians become, Jesus is still faithful.

Faithful Christians head in the right direction, following Jesus' roadmap. As they hurry toward their eternal destination, they seek to bring as many people as possible along with them. And though they don't live as perfectly as Christ, their message remains valid because it is His message, not theirs. As they travel, these believers are not relying on some imaginary hope. When they face troubles, they stand firm on the promise that nothing earthly will separate them from Him forever:

Who shall separate us from the love of Christ? Shall tribulation, or distress, or persecution, or famine, or nakedness, or danger, or sword? . . . . For I am sure that neither death nor life, nor angels nor rulers, nor things present nor things to come, nor powers, nor height nor depth, nor anything else in all creation, will be able to separate us from the love of God in Christ Jesus our Lord.

ROMANS 8:35, 38–39 ESV

Faith in Jesus is the center of the Christian life. Anyone who tries to accomplish anything apart from Him will surely fail.

Helped by the Spirit

Despite their imperfections, Christians can stand fast in the certainty of their connection to God, because their lives are infused by His Spirit. Jesus promised His disciples:

"If you love Me, keep My commandments. And I will pray the Father, and He will give you another Helper, that He may abide with you forever—the Spirit of truth, whom the world cannot receive, because it neither sees Him nor knows Him; but you know Him, for He dwells with you and will be in you."

JOHN 14:15–17 NKJV

Today He continues to send the Helper to those who trust in Him. The Spirit continues to indwell all authentic Christians, testifying to their connection with Him and leading them into a deeper experience of God. As they grow in God, their lives become more like their Master's.

Christians often have a hard time encouraging others to believe in Him because unbelievers do not have the Spirit and cannot understand what it means to have God in their lives. Faith is something that must be experienced to be fully appreciated. Only when God's Spirit works on the unbelieving heart will it begin to open to the truth about Him.

As the Spirit works, He works powerfully. Those who receive the Helper experience His strength in their lives. They are no longer totally sidelined by sin, because the Spirit fills them with God's wisdom and power. No longer do they make decisions based on frail human wisdom, because God directs their ways.

> *"When He, the Spirit of truth, has come, He will guide you into all truth; for He will not speak on His own authority, but whatever He hears He will speak; and He will tell you things to come. He will glorify Me, for He will take of what is Mine and declare it to you. All things that the Father has are Mine.*

Therefore I said that He will take of Mine and declare it to you."

JOHN 16:13–15 NKJV

Even the most average life, lived in Christ, is remarkable, because it is lived in the wisdom of God. The Spirit reveals the truths of God to believers, who have the mind of Christ working within them. Through His work in their lives, they know how to act and please their Master.

As it is written: "Eye has not seen, nor ear heard, nor have entered into the heart of man the things which God has prepared for those who love Him."

But God has revealed them to us through His Spirit. For the Spirit searches all things, yes, the deep things of God. For what man knows the things of a man except the spirit of the man which is in him? Even so no one knows the things of God except the Spirit of God. Now we have received, not the spirit of the world, but the Spirit who is from God, that we might know the things that have been freely given to us by God.

These things we also speak, not in words which man's wisdom teaches but which the Holy Spirit teaches, comparing spiritual things with spiritual. But the natural man does not receive the things of the Spirit of God, for they are foolishness to him; nor can he know them, because they are spiritually discerned. But he who is spiritual judges all things, yet he himself is rightly judged by no one. For "who has known the mind of the Lord that he may instruct Him?" But we have the mind of Christ.

1 CORINTHIANS 2:9–16 NKJV

Through His death for our sins, Jesus bought us back from sin and fulfilled the requirements of the law. But that is only the beginning of the gifts God has for those who live a Christian life. The work of the Holy Spirit brings us into a righteous life, enabling us to avoid the sin that still confronts us every day. Our spirits are enlivened by Him, and we live in resurrection power.

For what the law could not do in that it was weak through the flesh, God did by sending His own Son in the likeness of sinful flesh, on account of sin: He condemned sin in the flesh, that the righteous requirement of the law might be fulfilled in us who do not walk according to the flesh but according to the Spirit. For those who live according to the flesh set their minds on the things of the flesh, but those who live according to the Spirit, the things of the Spirit. For to be carnally minded is death, but to be spiritually minded is life and peace. Because the carnal mind is enmity against God; for it is not subject to the law of God, nor indeed can be. So then, those who are in the flesh cannot please God.

But you are not in the flesh but in the Spirit, if indeed the Spirit of God dwells in you. Now if anyone does not have the Spirit of Christ, he is not His. And if Christ is in you, the body is dead because of sin, but the Spirit is life because of righteousness. But if the Spirit of Him who raised Jesus from the dead dwells in you, He who raised Christ from the dead will also give life to your mortal bodies through His Spirit who dwells in you.

ROMANS 8:3–11 NKJV

This is eternal life as it appears here on earth.

How do we know we are in this kind of relationship with God? The Spirit Himself lets us know as He works in our hearts. By His testimony and the fact that God has kept His promise in John 16:13–15 that the Spirit will guide us into truth, we can believe that God will fulfill His promises for the future, too. Not only will He be with us on earth, we will be with Him in eternity as well:

The Spirit Himself bears witness with our spirit that we are children of God, and if children, then heirs—heirs of God and joint heirs with Christ, if indeed we suffer with Him, that we may also be glorified together.

ROMANS 8:16–17 NKJV

Knowing God, we have reason to hope for an eternity spent with Him.

Seeking Eternal Life

One man came to Jesus, seeking eternal life: "And behold, a man came up to him, saying, 'Teacher, what good deed must I do to have eternal life?' " (Matthew 19:16 ESV). Clearly, when this man asked Jesus that question, he expected Jesus to add some minor insight into the law he had been familiar with all his life—some key he had missed throughout an outwardly faithful life. Or maybe he expected commendation from the Master: "Oh you're doing just fine; you will certainly make it into heaven."

This rich young man got neither of those responses. Imagine his shock when, after reviewing some of the Ten Commandments, Jesus asked him to sell all his worldly goods and follow Him. He had not expected such a drastic request. The man walked away, sorrowful that he could not bring himself to give up his riches and perhaps disappointed that Jesus had asked so much of him. That decision impoverished him spiritually; he missed out on the opportunity not only to obey the law, but to have Jesus in his life for eternity.

This man missed out on the fact that God, not he, created the standards for spiritual life. Adding one good deed was not going to change the balance of his life. As Franklin Graham reminds us: "To have eternal life, we must relate to God on His terms, not ours. He is, after all, God. So, the test of any faith's validity is whether it conforms to His standard."

Jesus called this rich young man to give all he owned in this world, along with his heart, mind, and soul, in exchange for new life and eternity with Him. The man's soul balked because he was caught up in greed. He could not imagine that heavenly blessings could be greater than what he had in goods and money. Perhaps he had expected a minor tune-up in his spiritual life—a few more donations to the temple or a small change in how he worshipped. But Jesus asked him to give up everything he owned, and he wasn't willing to pay that price.

Jesus has never called any of His followers to access heaven by doing good deeds. All scripture tells us this is futile, yet people still try to do it and become confused when all the good deeds they can muster still aren't enough. The world tells us we're okay without repentance or that if we do 51 percent good and 49 percent wrong, God will let us into heaven. This is a lie from Satan.

Jesus does not change His standards to usher people into heaven—not even people He loves. Mark's Gospel tells us He loved that rich young man (see Mark 10:21). No one can buy heaven—with either actions or money. Even this prosperous man didn't have enough to gain heaven. Salvation is Jesus' gift, freely offered. But many people still want to accept it on their own terms.

God doesn't want halfhearted believers but fully committed followers. Trust in Him is an all-or-nothing matter. We can't trust in Him for 51 percent and something else for the other 49. Either we commit ourselves to fight sin and please Him, or we admit we don't want to believe and continue in our sinful ways.

Gaining Eternal Life

Speaking to Nicodemus, a member of the Jewish ruling council, Jesus described the covenant God wants to make with us and the consequences of avoiding commitment to Him:

> *"For God loved the world so much that he gave his one and only Son, so that everyone who believes in him will not perish but have*

eternal life. God sent his Son into the world not to judge the world, but to save the world through him.

"There is no judgment against anyone who believes in him. But anyone who does not believe in him has already been judged for not believing in God's one and only Son. And the judgment is based on this fact: God's light came into the world, but people loved the darkness more than the light, for their actions were evil. All who do evil hate the light and refuse to go near it for fear their sins will be exposed. But those who do what is right come to the light so others can see that they are doing what God wants."

JOHN 3:16–21 NLT

In Bible times, a covenant was an agreement between two parties, one more powerful than the other. Often it was between a conquering king and the people over whom he had won a battle. Each party was bound to do certain things, which were defined in the covenant. God, being the greater party to this covenant, gave the most—the life of His Son—and promised to reward those who trusted in Him with eternal life (see 1 John 2:25; 5:11).

According to this covenant, every person must have an allegiance to God. Those who accept His salvation live in His light; those who do not accept Him will live eternally in the darkness, far from Him.

God the Father gave Jesus the authority to give eternal life to those who trust in Him. No one can bypass Him or offer their allegiance to another and still have the life He offers:

> *"For you granted him authority over all people that he might give eternal life to all those you have given him. Now this is eternal life: that they know you, the only true God, and Jesus Christ, whom you have sent."*
>
> John 17:2–3 niv

Many people do not like to hear this. To them, it's not good news at all. They would prefer to make God suit their own ideas, rather than relating to Him on His terms. Instead of following Jesus they prefer a more conformable god who suits their lifestyles. They complain that Christians are so narrow-minded as to require everyone to agree with them. Is it narrow-mindedness to tell the truth and want others to join you on its path? In calling others to choose life in Christ, Christians are offering others the opportunity to live with Him in eternity. They are recognizing the truth and trying to draw others to it, too.

Those who come to God on His own terms find their lives transformed. Based on His work on the cross, they are able to begin to live the righteous lives they needed to live all along (see Galatians 6:8). Their righteousness problem has been solved.

Living in Righteousness

Paul described God's gift of salvation and the life he lived after he met Jesus on the road to Damascus:

> *I thank him who has given me strength, Christ Jesus our Lord, because he judged me faithful, appointing me to his service, though formerly I was a blasphemer, persecutor, and insolent opponent. But I received mercy because I had acted ignorantly in unbelief, and the grace of our Lord overflowed for me with the faith and love that are in Christ Jesus. The saying is trustworthy and deserving of full acceptance, that Christ Jesus came into the world to save sinners, of whom I am the foremost. But I received mercy for this reason, that in me, as the foremost, Jesus Christ might display his perfect patience as an example to those who were to believe in him for eternal life.*
>
> 1 Timothy 1:12–16 ESV

God saved Paul for a purpose and gave him a ministry that stretched around the Mediterranean world. God had promised eternal life to His people well before Paul or any of his fellow apostles were born (see Titus 1:2–3). Amazingly, He entrusted the message of salvation to one of His worst former enemies, a man who once persecuted Christians with zeal. God's forgiveness was complete and life changing for Paul.

Today, it's no different for us. Though we rebelled against God and even became involved in terrible wickedness, God still wants to give us a bright, new relationship with Himself. And just as He gave kingdom work to Paul, God entrusts each of His newborn children with ministries with which they can serve Him.

The Christian life is not a matter of sitting around doing nothing. Active service is required. And it starts immediately. God is building a whole new person, and our service in His kingdom should shape us day after day into the people He wants us to be. There is a world out there that needs to hear the Good News of salvation, and each new believer has a part in this proclamation.

Turning from Sin

Another part of this new Christian life is to resist the sin that so easily entangles us. From the very first, God called people to do this—as He told Adam and Eve not to eat of one specific tree in the garden. When anger threatened to overwhelm Cain, God warned him: "If you do well, will you not be accepted? And if you do not do well, sin lies at the door. And its desire is for you, but you should rule over it" (Genesis 4:7 NKJV).

The prophet Isaiah called his countrymen to turn from sin. Speaking for God, he told the nation of Judah:

> *"Wash yourselves, make yourselves clean; put away the evil of your doings from before My eyes. Cease to do evil, learn to do good; seek justice, rebuke the oppressor; defend the fatherless, plead for the widow."*
>
> Isaiah 1:16–17 NKJV

The newborn Christian has a whole new relationship with sin—he can fight back against it, and in God's power, overcome it. The apostle James's portrayal of God's call to resist sin adds two promises of victory: The devil will flee from the resisting Christian, and God will lift up those who resist:

> *Therefore submit to God. Resist the devil and he will flee from you. Draw near to God and He will draw near to you. Cleanse your hands,*

you sinners; and purify your hearts, you double-minded. Lament and mourn and weep! Let your laughter be turned to mourning and your joy to gloom. Humble yourselves in the sight of the Lord, and He will lift you up.

James 4:7–10 NKJV

English Puritan Richard Baxter advised Christians to take sin seriously, fighting back against its power, because sin harms both them and their Lord:

Use sin as it will use you; spare it not, for it will not spare you; it is your murderer, and the murderer of the world: use it, therefore, as a murderer should be used. Kill it before it kills you; and though it bring you to the grave, as it did your Head, it shall not be able to keep you there.

By submitting to God's will and resisting sin, we give His Spirit freedom to work in our lives and to defeat Satan—something we are incapable of doing on our own. Our new life in Christ begins with forgiveness, which God has done for all our sin—past, present, and future. But though He will woo us into obedience and even place us in situations where we cannot ignore our sin, He will not force us into compliance in our daily lives. Though He offers victory, we can still choose to live in defeat.

The Christian life is not so much instant perfection as it is the start of a race (see Hebrews 12:1). We work out our salvation day by day (see Philippians 2:12), and this means to resist the sin that continues to dog our footsteps.

The good news is that sin is already conquered in Jesus, and we can resist Satan effectively. Though sin may enter our lives, it need not fully control them.

The "Eternity" in Eternal Life

All people do both good and wicked things. After we draw our last breaths, we will go to our rewards—we eternally join the one whom we have served and trusted in on earth. Christians will see God's promise of salvation confirmed:

> *Do you not know that all of us who have been baptized into Christ Jesus were baptized into his death? We were buried therefore with him by baptism into death, in order that, just as Christ was raised from the dead by the glory of the Father, we too might walk in newness of life.*
>
> *For if we have been united with him in a death like his, we shall certainly be united with him in a resurrection like his. We know*

that our old self was crucified with him in order that the body of sin might be brought to nothing, so that we would no longer be enslaved to sin. For one who has died has been set free from sin.

Romans 6:3–7 ESV

"The amazing center of the Good News is this," Ron Hutchcraft admits, "I did the sinning; Jesus did the dying. Because of Him, we can trade in a death penalty we deserve for eternal life we don't deserve."

But those who have not known Jesus' resurrection power in their own lives have chosen eternal death with His enemy. "Choose any life but the life of God and heaven, and you choose death, for death is nothing else but the loss of the life of God," William Law warned.

The Bible confirms this, comparing the lives of those who reject Him and those who come to Him in faith:

For those who are self-seeking and do not obey the truth, but obey unrighteousness, there will be wrath and fury. There will be tribulation and distress for every human being who does evil, the Jew first and also the Greek, but glory and honor and peace for everyone who does good, the Jew first and also the Greek.

For God shows no partiality.

Romans 2:8–11 ESV

But isn't it unfair, some people will ask, to deny heaven to anyone? Christopher Love has it right when he declares: "If the Lord should bring a wicked man to heaven, heaven would be hell to him; for he who loves not grace upon earth will never love it in heaven." Heaven is a place where God is glorified, and anyone who does not love Him will not want to be there. We make our choices on earth, and heaven allows us to live the life we chose for all eternity.

CHAPTER 5
Christ and Sinners

But God demonstrates his own love for us in this:
While we were still sinners, Christ died for us.
ROMANS 5:8 NIV

We were truly down-and-out, unable to get our wheels on the road. Worse than that, by most people's standards we didn't even deserve help. We weren't heading in a good direction, nor did we have an important mission before us. In fact, we may have been going somewhere "good" people don't go. Of ourselves, we seemingly had no value. Yet just at that moment, when we were least deserving, just as our hubcaps began to disappear under the muck, and it seemed as if we would be eaten alive by the mire, God stepped into our lives with a solution to our problem: "For while we were still weak, at the right time Christ died for the ungodly" (Romans 5:6 ESV).

The Bible admits the depth of God's love by declaring, "For one will scarcely die for a righteous person—though perhaps for a good person one would dare even to die" (Romans 5:7 ESV). Then our verse for this chapter describes the depths of God's love in doing just that.

At the very moment when we most needed a solution and could do the least to help ourselves, God gave Himself for us. The sin we could not escape or eradicate He took upon Himself. Though He was perfect, not deserving of death, Jesus willingly gave up His earthly life.

As He gave up His righteous life, an amazing exchange took place: those who accepted that He had died in their place, for their sins, received His life for their old, mucky place of death.

The Love of a Righteous God

Here is a righteous God—One who values people, despite their wrongdoing and sheer wrongheadedness, who freely forgives all those who recognize their sin and accept the redemption He calls them to:

> *And [we] are justified by his grace as a gift, through the redemption that is in Christ Jesus, whom God put forward as a propitiation by his blood, to be received by faith. This was to show God's righteousness, because in his divine forbearance he had passed over former sins. It was to show his righteousness at the*

present time, so that he might be just and the justifier of the one who has faith in Jesus.

ROMANS 3:24–26 ESV

Though we could not reach out to Him, God was reaching out to draw us into His kingdom. Love reached down in the form of Jesus. God sent His divine Son in the form of a man, so we might begin to understand His desire to relate to us.

This is how God showed his love among us: He sent his one and only Son into the world that we might live through him. This is love: not that we loved God, but that he loved us and sent his Son as an atoning sacrifice for our sins.

1 JOHN 4:9–10 NIV

God made His love concrete so we could understand it more fully. Jesus is a picture to all humanity of how much God the Father cares for us. Throughout the Old Testament, God spoke through the prophets. He provided information about Himself and the behavior He expected of His people. But with Jesus, humanity could see just what God was like.

Jesus' tenderness and gentleness showed everyone just how much God cared; His firmness showed them that He was serious about sin and its consequences. As He lived on earth, those who saw Him began to understand the complexities of God's nature and His love for people. Finally, Jesus fulfilled the law by paying the price for sin that mankind could not pay.

It is difficult for us to understand the incredible grace of an awesome, powerful God. He has no real need of us and could simply have taken us at our word and let us all live forever without Him. But His willingness to put up with our frailty is amazing. Not only does this merciful God put up with us in our weakness, but He loves us deeply and wants to make us righteous so we can love Him, too. This has been His aim all along, and He stopped at nothing to make it happen. Giving the life of His Son was not too much for Him. He gave and gave generously so we could join Him in heaven.

Even before Jesus stepped foot on earth, God was leading people into such a relationship with Him: "Abram believed the LORD, and he credited it to him as righteousness" (Genesis 15:6 NIV). The Old Testament is the story of those who believed—and numerous people who rebelled against Him. But even all those centuries ago, the world was looking forward to the coming of Jesus, and those who trusted in God were credited with righteousness on His account (see Galatians 3:6).

That's how righteousness, which once seemed unattainable, became the hallmark of those people who follow Him, the standard that sets believers apart from those who do not trust in Him. Those who were not righteous are made righteous. They have been so changed that scripture describes them with that word:

> *Consider how, in the word, the servants of God are praised as righteous (Genesis 6:9; 7:1; Matthew 1:19; Luke 1:6; 2:25; 2 Peter 2:7); how the favor and blessing of God are pronounced upon the righteous (Psalms 1:6; 5:13; 14:5; 34:16, 20; 37:17, 39; 92:13; 97:11; 144:8); how the righteous are called to confidence, to joy (Psalms 32:11; 33:1; 58:11; 64:11; 68:4; 97:12). See this especially in the Book of Psalms. See how in Proverbs, although you should take but one chapter only, all blessing is pronounced upon the righteous (Proverbs 10:3, 6, 7, 11, 16, 20, 21, 24, 25, 28, 30, 31, 32). See how everywhere men are divided into two classes, the righteous and the godless (Ecclesiastes 3:17; Isaiah 3:10; Ezekiel 3:18, 20; 18:21, 23; 33:12; Malachi 3:18; Matthew 5:45; 12:49; 25:46). See how, in the New Testament, the Lord Jesus demands this righteousness (Matthew 5:6,*

> *20; 6:33); how Paul, who announces most the doctrine of justification by faith alone, insists that this is the aim of justification, to form righteous men, who do right (Romans 3:31; 6:13, 22; 7:4, 6; 8:4; 2 Corinthians 9:9, 10; Philippians 1:11; 1 Timothy 6:11). See how John names righteousness along with love as the two indispensable marks of the children of God (1 John 2:4, 11, 29; 3:10; 5:2). When you put all these facts together, it must be very evident to you that a true Christian is a man who does righteous in all things, even as God is righteous.*
>
> ANDREW MURRAY

God's Enemies

Remember that when God offered us reconciliation with Himself, we were not just indifferent to Him. We were His enemies:

> *You. . .were once far away from God. You were his enemies, separated from him by your evil thoughts and actions. Yet now he has reconciled you to himself through the death of Christ in his physical body. As a result, he has brought you into his own presence, and you are holy and blameless as you stand before him without a single fault.*
>
> COLOSSIANS 1:21–22 NLT

Some of us—the terrorists of unbelievers—may have been more stubbornly opposed to Him than others. Like Saul the Pharisee, we may actively have sought to keep people from following Jesus or to punish those who insisted on doing so. Others of us may simply have ignored His claims on our lives. No matter how we opposed Him, we all raised our weapons of sin against Him.

As with Saul, who later became the apostle Paul, God did not ask us to put down our weapons before He would consider coming to our aid. Jesus confronted us when we least expected it, as we were going about the business of being His enemy.

Before each of us stood the One who gave Himself over to His opponents without complaint so He could reconcile us to God. The Father "made Him who knew no sin to be sin for us, that we might become the righteousness of God in Him" (2 Corinthians 5:21 NKJV). Like Paul, we may have seen God in His awesome power. Or we may have felt a gentle, wooing touch on our souls. But He confronted our need for Him and called us to Himself. Face-to-face with God, we could no longer avoid His call or escape into our own faithless ways of thinking.

Reconciliation with God

Jesus' death was not simply for the benefit of those who had followed Him for the three years of His ministry—the men who were closest to Him and first heard and responded to His message—or even for the crowds who heard His words and followed Him. You didn't have to be healed by His hand during His years on earth in order to receive reconciliation with God. Jesus' sacrifice was for all sinners throughout the centuries—all who needed reconciliation with God. Jesus was God's peacemaker for *all* mankind.

Jesus' once-for-all sacrifice reaches back in time to save those who believed in God under the law and reaches forward to the present, to save those who are still living. He is our only hope: "There is salvation in no one else! God has given no other name under heaven by which we must be saved" (Acts 4:12 NLT).

All of us, no matter where or when we have lived, have been God's enemies. But if we come to Him in faith, we benefit from that one day when He was sacrificed on the cross—and the day when He returned to life again, in the Resurrection:

> *For God in all his fullness was pleased to live in Christ, and through him God reconciled everything to himself. He made peace with everything in heaven and on earth by means of Christ's blood on the cross. This includes you who were once far away from God. You*

were his enemies, separated from him by your evil thoughts and actions. Yet now he has reconciled you to himself through the death of Christ in his physical body. As a result, he has brought you into his own presence, and you are holy and blameless as you stand before him without a single fault.

COLOSSIANS 1:19–22 NLT

As peacemaker, Jesus does more than stop our battle with God while we are on earth. He ends it forever, totally changing our allegiance in this world and bringing us into His eternal kingdom. Once we accept His gift of salvation, we delight in Him. This is the exact opposite of our former attitude of hostility.

For if when we were enemies we were reconciled to God through the death of His Son, much more, having been reconciled, we shall be saved by His life. And not only that, but we also rejoice in God through our Lord Jesus Christ, through whom we have now received the reconciliation.

ROMANS 5:10–11 NKJV

Through Jesus' death and the Resurrection that enables Him to give us new life, we have been saved from sin, both here on earth and for eternity. As Christians on earth, we are able to resist sin in His power. And because He makes us holy and blameless, we will spend eternity in heaven with Him when we die, glorifying the One who saved us.

Yet this new life in Christ is not just "pie in the sky by and by." It affects our daily lives, beginning the very minute we accept Him. As our hearts are changed and we begin to live to please God, we start to live differently. Sometimes our new outlook on life will be sheer pleasure, sometimes a serious struggle. But either way, we become aware that we need to follow God's will. We have a part in bringing God's peace to the world.

Paul describes the creation of a new person in Christ and the reconciliation that occurs with new life in Him. Then he looks forward to the ministry God places in believers' hands, calling us God's ambassadors.

> *Therefore, if anyone is in Christ, the new creation has come: The old has gone, the new is here! All this is from God, who reconciled us to himself through Christ and gave us the ministry of reconciliation: that God was reconciling the world to himself in Christ, not counting people's sins against them. And he has committed to us the message of reconciliation. We*

are therefore Christ's ambassadors, as though God were making his appeal through us. We implore you on Christ's behalf: Be reconciled to God. God made him who had no sin to be sin for us, so that in him we might become the righteousness of God.

2 Corinthians 5:17–21 NIV

The Christian life is one of reconciliation—both of those within the church and those who need to be reconciled to Christ by starting a relationship with Him.

The church is not a congregation of perfect people, and we sometimes need to work out reconciliations within the members of His body, the church. It was true in Paul's time, and it's true today as well. In his work as an apostle, Paul, a Jew, had seen opposition between his own people and Gentiles in congregations. But he also knew that in Jesus, both were brothers, meant to live in peace.

Together as one body, Christ reconciled both groups [Jews and Gentiles] to God by means of his death on the cross, and our hostility toward each other was put to death. He brought this Good News of peace to you Gentiles who were far away from him, and peace to the Jews who were near.

Ephesians 2:16–17 NLT

For the church to be effective in its ministry to the world, brothers and sisters must work together in peace. When troubles arise, they need to be dealt with quickly, before they turn into monsters that destroy congregations and hurt other believers. And every Christian is responsible for keeping the peace.

Jesus won't allow the unreconciled condition to continue among believers. In Matthew 5, if another considers you to have wronged him, Jesus says that you must go. In Matthew 18, He says that if the other person has done something wrong to you, you must go. There is never a time when you can sit and wait for your brother to come to you. Jesus doesn't allow for that. He gives no opportunity for that. It is always your obligation to go.

JAY E. ADAMS

But the message of peace with God is not something we hold on to for ourselves and other believers. This wonderful truth is that the God who is our friend is also meant to be shared with the rest of the world. God uses us to reach out to others whom He would also save—those who have yet to hear and respond to His Good News.

As Christ came to earth so that we could understand God in a concrete way, we become His representatives in the lives of those around us. To fulfill that role, we need to share with others their need of salvation. Often people don't accept this message, but we continue to persevere in telling others about Him. Why? Paul explains the motivation:

> *For we must all appear before the judgment seat of Christ, so that each of us may receive what is due us for the things done while in the body, whether good or bad. Since, then, we know what it is to fear the Lord, we try to persuade others.*
>
> 2 CORINTHIANS 5:10–11 NIV

We as believers are not concerned with pleasing the world, but pleasing our Master. He has told us to share the gospel with others, so we speak out, write the truth, and use every possible method to keep others from missing out on the greatest truth they will ever know.

Though good works cannot earn heaven for us, God judges His own people according to what they have done on earth as they have sought to serve Him. As we seek to please our Master, we obey Him—and that includes sharing our faith with those who are in need of Him. He has called us to make disciples and teach them everything He commands (see Matthew 28:19–20).

Our Response to God's Grace

When we recognize all that Jesus gave up for us and all the Father has done to reconcile us to Himself, we as believers give thanks for His goodness and mercy. But a truly thankful Christian also takes that feeling and understanding to heart and puts them into action.

> *Christ also suffered for us, leaving us an example, that you should follow His steps: "Who committed no sin, nor was deceit found in His mouth"; who, when He was reviled, did not revile in return; when He suffered, He did not threaten, but committed Himself to Him who judges righteously; who Himself bore our sins in His own body on the tree, that we, having died to sins, might live for righteousness—by whose stripes you were healed.*
>
> 1 PETER 2:21–24 NKJV

> *Everyone who sins breaks the law; in fact, sin is lawlessness. But you know that he appeared so that he might take away our sins. And in him is no sin. No one who lives in him keeps on sinning. No one who continues to sin has either seen him or known him.*
>
> 1 JOHN 3:4–6 NIV

People of faith are also people of action. They devote their lives to worship of their Lord by seeking to do everything He has commanded them to do. As they grow in their knowledge of what God has done for them, their lives reflect His glory more and more. Drawing nearer to God through the power of the Spirit, they increasingly turn aside from sin. Not to do so would be to take His sacrifice lightly.

Jesus did not die so we could live sloppy Christian lives, obeying Him when we feel like it and ignoring Him when we had rather go another way. If we are heading for eternity, we need to be ready to live with God. Those who render great service for God's kingdom while on earth will be best prepared for the joys of heaven.

By giving up His earthly life, Jesus placed our wheels back on a new, perfect road that heads in a heavenly direction. Just as it is expensive to build a new four-lane highway, putting us back on the right road was a costly proposition for God. But He spent more than we would for a multi-billion-dollar highway—for His Son spent more than thirty years on earth when He could have lived in comfort in heaven. Then the very people He had come to save offered Him only a gruesome death by crucifixion.

But God did not begrudge any of it. The price

was worth it to Him because it brought about the reconciliation between God and man that His heart desired.

CHAPTER 6
The Commitment of Salvation

If you declare with your mouth, "Jesus is Lord," and believe in your heart that God raised him from the dead, you will be saved. For it is with your heart that you believe and are justified, and it is with your mouth that you profess your faith and are saved.
ROMANS 10:9–10 NIV

Our modern Adam's salvation seems so simple, if you take a good look at Romans 10:9. Speaking the right words and believing in Jesus—that's all it seems to take. One could be fooled into thinking that accepting Jesus is a matter of glib words with little meaning. But recognize that declaring faith in Jesus is much more than easy words or a smooth exercise of the tongue. In this verse God isn't maintaining that any person who just mouths the words "Jesus is Lord" spends eternity with Him. This is not a matter of "fire insurance" faith that can slip a person inside the heavenly portal without anything more than a few words. There is no such thing in the Bible.

Any acceptance of Christ that has no real commitment behind it will make no difference in a person's eternal destination. Walking down an aisle or just praying a rote prayer will not get you into heaven. Nor can anyone start a relationship with God simply by saying the words "Jesus is Lord" by accident. The "and" in Romans 10:9 is supremely important. To be saved from sin, our modern Adam and others must *both* speak words of faith in Jesus, declaring that He rules their lives, *and* believe this in their hearts. Those three little words reflect a deep heart change that has already occurred. Romans 10:10 goes on to make this clear, as it reverses the two ideas, putting acceptance in one's heart before the verbal confession of Jesus' lordship.

Nor is biblical faith a matter of believing in a myth or fairy tale. With those words the new believer is reaching out to God, telling Him, "You made these promises in Your Word, Lord, and I am trusting that they are true, that You are who You say you are, and that You will keep Your promises." This trust is not in something without substance, but in the real, living God described in the Bible.

The God behind the Faith

If we have placed our trust in Jesus alone, we need not fear that we have somehow spoken the wrong words or done something wrong and missed out on salvation. When our hearts believe in Him and we declare our faith, He will keep His part of the promise. Though people may fail, He cannot. Many people think they and their confession are the critical part of the salvation equation, but it's not true. The most important element of the Christian faith is not the person who professes it but the God who stands behind it.

> *Some say faith is merely believing certain facts. One popular Bible teacher says saving faith is nothing more than confidence in the divine offer of eternal life.*
>
> *Biblically, however, the object of faith is not the divine offer; it is the Person of Jesus Christ. Faith in Him is what saves, not just believing His promises or accepting facts about Him. Saving faith has to be more than accepting facts. Even demons have that kind of faith (see James 2:19).*
>
> John MacArthur

Promises are not what save us—Jesus is. Yet as we read the scriptures, we see that God has already kept His promises. From the early part of Genesis, He told of a Savior who would undo the sin that Adam and Eve started in the world when they fell for Satan's lies (see Genesis 3:15). God fulfilled that promise two thousand years ago when He sent His Son to earth. Jesus was the Promised One who would crush the head of Satan, destroying the power of sin over humanity. The Old Testament had foretold His coming to forgive sin (see Isaiah 7:14; 53:4–6; 59:20), and He accomplished that through the cross and His resurrection. By His promises, we see that God has been faithful before, and we trust that He will be faithful in those things He has promised for our lives.

Christians believe "God raised [Jesus] from the dead" in the Resurrection. He lived a sinless life and was sacrificed in their place. They deserved to die and didn't, because He took their punishment so they could live anew in Him. His death and resurrection occurred so God could forgive their sins and bring them to new life. Just like Abraham, who trusted in God's promises and had that faith counted as righteousness (see Romans 4:3), Christians today have their faith applied to God's promise of redemption, and their sins are also forgiven.

Those who trust in Him now look forward to an eternal reward they have yet to see. None of this—salvation in this life or the next—is some kind of celestial magic, but the completion of God's promise. Christians trust in Him—not just in some memorized promises or the facts they have learned about Him. And as they believe, He completes the promise by saving them.

Heartfelt Faith

The heartfelt belief Paul speaks of in Romans 10:9 is not an intellectual assent or a faint feeling or hope that "maybe this is true." Knowledge that Jesus is who He said He was rocks the soul as He confronts us with our need of Him and offers us new life. Though He may speak gently to the hurting, needy soul and woo it into His kingdom, even those who come gently recognize that He is still incredibly powerful, the Lord of glory, Creator of the earth. Those who want a comfortable, "gentle Jesus meek and mild" have experienced only a pale picture of Him that cannot compare to the real, powerful Lord who works His changes in human lives.

Guilt-wracked Martin Luther was not looking for a comfortable God. He was seeking a real solution to his own sin problem. So he looked for God within the church, becoming a monk and rigorously denying himself every pleasure of life. Yet sin still bore down on him. Nothing seemed to solve his desire for holiness and his inability to achieve it. Luther constantly confessed his sin, to the dismay of his confessor, but he could never please his own sense of the need for righteousness in his life. He finally realized he lived in fear of this deity he had hoped to serve.

Several years after that realization, as professor of biblical theology at the University of

Wittenberg, Luther prepared to lecture on the book of Romans. One day the zealous but dissatisfied monk ran straight into Romans 1:17 (KJV): "For therein is the righteousness of God revealed from faith to faith: as it is written, The just shall live by faith."

The last six words rang in Luther's spirit—suddenly he had the answer he had been seeking for years. Faith was all he needed to be righteous. He experienced what Paul tells us about in Romans 10:10—that with real heart faith, the believer is justified (or made right with God). Luther found himself no longer separated from God by sin.

Finally Luther knew how he and others could relate to a God who demanded a level of righteousness no human could provide. Later, he wrote:

> *Faith is a work of God in us, which changes us and brings us to birth anew from God (cf. John 1). It kills the old Adam, makes us completely different people in heart, mind, senses, and all our powers, and brings the Holy Spirit with it. What a living, creative, active powerful thing is faith! It is impossible that faith ever stop doing good. Faith doesn't ask whether good works are to be done, but, before it is asked, it has done them.*

Martin Luther's faith went on to change the world as he confronted the church of that day about its lack of biblical teaching. Excommunicated from the Catholic Church, he founded a new Protestant denomination that still bears his name. Yet the focus of this new church was not Luther, but the Bible that had helped him understand his need for Christ through faith. Luther and his fellow Protestant leaders fanned the flames of desire for a personal, biblical relationship with God that had begun to burn throughout Europe. Out of this fire came the Reformation, which changed the face of European Christianity and led many people to choose an intensely personal faith founded on God's Word.

John Gill describes the kind of heartfelt faith God expects of His people in these words:

> *It is heart work, a believing with all the heart; such a faith in which all the powers of the soul, the understanding, will, and affections, are concerned, it is a seeing of the Son, a beholding of the glory, fulness, suitableness, ability, and willingness of Christ as a Savior, with the eye of the understanding spiritually enlightened; it is a going out of the soul to Christ, in various acts, such as venturing into His presence, prostrating itself at His feet, resolving if it perishes it will perish there; a*

> *giving up itself unto him, determining it will have no other Savior, leaning and relying on Him, and living upon Him; which faith works by love to Christ, moves the affections, stirs up the desires of the soul to His name, and endears Him and all that belong to Him to it.*

Nothing is left out of such faith. Nothing is denied to the Savior, because the new believer trusts in Him for every part of the future. Such a person is surely saved.

A Resurrection Faith

God's Word tells us that this saving faith must trust that God raised Jesus from the dead. *What does that mean?* some people may wonder. *Why is this death any different from any other? And why should it have anything to do with me?*

When the apostle Peter gave his first sermon, he told the Jewish people:

> *"God raised [Jesus] from the dead, freeing him from the agony of death, because it was impossible for death to keep its hold on him. . . . [The patriarch David] spoke of the resurrection of the Messiah, that he was not abandoned to the realm of the dead, nor did his body see decay. God has raised this Jesus to*

life, and we are all witnesses of it. Exalted to the right hand of God, he has received from the Father the promised Holy Spirit and has poured out what you now see and hear. . . .

"Therefore let all Israel be assured of this: God has made this Jesus, whom you crucified, both Lord and Messiah."

Acts 2:24, 31–33, 36 NIV

Jesus, Peter informed the Jews, was their long-awaited Messiah—God's chosen ruler, whom the Old Testament foretold would be a son of David and their King and Redeemer (see Isaiah 9:6; Job 19:25). This was the man they had awaited for many centuries—the deliverer who would free them from their enemies and the sin that entrapped them (see Isaiah 53:4–6; 59:15–20). God had promised, and He fulfilled that promise when He sent the Promised One.

But many of the Jews expected the Messiah to be more of a political figure—an earthly deliverer who would save them from the rule of the Roman Empire—than someone who was important to their spiritual lives. They missed out on the fact that the blood of the animal sacrifices they had made for so long was simply symbolic of Jesus' sacrifice on the cross.

Jesus' death was different because of who He

is—very God of very God—and the mission God sent Him on—to save souls by being made an innocent sacrifice whose blood could cover the sins of those who trusted in Him. No one else could have done that.

The book of Romans makes it clear that the Messiah, or Christ, is of extreme importance to the personal faith of those who trust in Him—both Jew and Gentile, since the church in Rome was made up of God's ancient people and those He had grafted in (see Romans 11). Christianity isn't an idea to give assent to but a personal choice about whom we put our trust in and how we live our lives.

Jesus' resurrection makes a new, holy life possible for those who trust in Him. Because the grave could not hold Him, we are saved from our sins, we are empowered to live the righteous lives God calls us to, and we have the promise of eternal life with Him. Instead of dying eternally, we are raised to a new eternal life. The Bible pictures this in baptism.

> *Or have you forgotten that when we were joined with Christ Jesus in baptism, we joined him in his death? For we died and were buried with Christ by baptism. And just as Christ was raised from the dead by the glorious power of the Father, now we also may live new lives.*

Since we have been united with him in his death, we will also be raised to life as he was.

ROMANS 6:3–5 NLT

As we are raised to new life in Jesus, we are filled with God's Spirit, who raised Him from the dead. We experience a wonderful spiritual event in which God enters our spirits, and even our mortal bodies are affected by our new life. Our physical bodies will one day be transformed, too (see Philippians 3:21).

The Spirit of God, who raised Jesus from the dead, lives in you. And just as God raised Christ Jesus from the dead, he will give life to your mortal bodies by this same Spirit living within you.

ROMANS 8:11 NLT

The death and resurrection of Jesus has everything to do with faith and new life in Him. The Resurrection proved that Jesus was who He claimed to be. He was not just an interesting new prophet who had something to say about God; He was the One whom God the Father had sent to conquer the spiritual death that held mankind in its grip.

Express mention is made only of Christ's resurrection; which must not be so taken, as though His death was of no moment, but because Christ, by rising again, completed the whole work of our salvation: for though redemption and satisfaction were effected by His death, through which we are reconciled to God; yet the victory over sin, death, and Satan was attained by His resurrection; and hence also came righteousness, newness of life, and the hope of a blessed immortality. And thus is resurrection alone often set before us as the assurance of our salvation, not to draw away our attention from His death, but because it bears witness to the efficacy and fruit of His death: in short, His resurrection includes His death.

John Calvin

Not only did Jesus live again for Himself, He completely changed the lives of those who trust in Him. They would never again be the same old sin-bound people. They became brand-new people with a new focus in life—Jesus and the ability to live for Him. His death and resurrection are critical elements of faith for all people who are confronted with God's claims on their lives. They have seen the change (and often others have, too) and are sharing that change with others.

A Picture of New Life

So that we can understand what happens in our lives when we accept Jesus as our Lord, God has given us the physical picture of adult baptism. Baptism portrays the death of the old person and the rebirth that God has provided. As the new Christian goes into the water, it shows the death of the old person and his previous sinful way of life. The baptized believer arises from the water to new life—a completely changed person, not just a slightly cleaner and wetter version of the old one.

All the pictures of what Christ has done for us are just that—pictures. Though they can help us understand what is going on in the human spirit as a result of rebirth, they are only faint descriptions of the joy of the new birth and the spiritual realities they describe. Nothing is as wonderful as a clean soul that is free to worship God and turn from sin. And a new relationship with God—one that becomes deeper every day—cannot be described with words. Those who have not known the joy of Jesus cannot imagine what a wonderful life they are missing.

The Cost of Faith

Though putting faith in Jesus is wonderfully beneficial, believing in your heart comes with a great cost. God gives the gift of His Son freely, but this new life requires a serious commitment because it also demands much of the person who accepts it. Faith that doesn't expect a good deal from the believer is not the real thing, because God doesn't give His beloved ones anything cheap.

Costly Christianity is not popular. Jesus and His message go counter to the world's values by insisting that God, not man, is the first consideration in the believer's life. Nor are selfishness and self-indulgence Christian virtues. Jesus is countercultural. Living an extraordinary, faithful life may become uncomfortable for believers at times.

The Lord pointed this out when He told the crowds who followed Him:

> *"If anyone comes to me and does not hate his own father and mother and wife and children and brothers and sisters, yes, and even his own life, he cannot be my disciple. Whoever does not bear his own cross and come after me cannot be my disciple. For which of you, desiring to build a tower, does not first sit down and count the cost, whether he has enough to complete it?"*
>
> Luke 14:26–28 ESV

When Jesus told the crowd they must hate their family members, He was not advocating familial warfare; He was pointing out the unpopularity of choosing God. How many Christians have made their commitment because Jesus pulled at their hearts, only to experience the severe displeasure of family members? Throwing in the towel is not an option in such a situation, even though new Christians may feel the pain of family disapproval.

Those who stand firm in their faith, despite objections, and trust in their Lord will find His support lifting them up and leading them to become witnesses to their families. And it will challenge the faith of new believers, leading them to trust Jesus in all circumstances.

This need for real commitment is part of why no one can fool you into becoming a Christian by making you speak the words "Jesus is Lord." God will never drag people, kicking and screaming, into His heaven. Taking Jesus as Lord is a serious commitment that needs to be carefully considered. To accept Jesus' rule is a life-changing and demanding choice. The person who declares that Jesus is Lord must believe that those words are true and that He has the power to change their lives. Then the new Christian must be willing to have God work in his life, no matter what the cost.

Jesus takes those words of faith very seriously, because they determine a person's eternal future. Anyone who denies Jesus will in turn be denied by Him.

> *"Whoever acknowledges me before others, I will also acknowledge before my Father in heaven. But whoever disowns me before others, I will disown before my Father in heaven."*
>
> MATTHEW 10:32–33 NIV

To acknowledge Jesus with both words and a committed life is the key to acceptance into heaven (see John 3:17–18). Anyone who disowns Him before others denies Him before God, as well, and cannot gain a place in eternity with Him. Our mouths and actions show clearly what is in our hearts.

Traveling the Romans Road

Whether or not we recognize it, all of us are offered a choice about the road we take in our lives. At some point we will have had an invitation to walk on the Romans Road, a road that requires us to confront the kind of faith described in the Bible. A person may share his faith with us for just a few minutes or we may read of it in a book or magazine. Though it may take only a few minutes, this is still God's offer of redemption placed before us. Will we accept it or turn from it?

Jesus freely offers us this new road of faith in Him. But after we've chosen it, we need to follow the new road map that He provides in His Word, the Bible. Otherwise, we will just sit on the side of this new road and won't have much of a faith life. We'll simply park ourselves by the roadside, right near the ditch He pulled us out of. After a while we may wonder what all the excitement was about, as we don't seem to experience the exciting life we expected. We may never realize that we've been sidelined spiritually. That wasn't the way God intended His people to live.

Accompanying Jesus on His new road requires us to be committed to His final destination, to keep traveling, and to make all the turns the road requires. It may not always be an easy road. We may face snowstorms, downpours, and traffic jams, but we can still travel on the right highway, knowing that we're headed in the right direction. If we put Jesus in charge of our journey, our heavenly destination will always be before us. We'll have hope throughout our lives, no matter how difficult they become.

Counting the Cost

Since Jesus advises us to count the cost before we believe, let's take a look at what it means to travel down this Romans Road. Paul reminds us that the death and resurrection of Jesus are a picture of our renewed lives in Him and of the ongoing changes that need to occur in our lives:

For the death he died he died to sin, once for all, but the life he lives he lives to God. So you also must consider yourselves dead to sin and alive to God in Christ Jesus.

Let not sin therefore reign in your mortal body, to make you obey its passions. Do not present your members to sin as instruments for unrighteousness, but present yourselves to God as those who have been brought from death to life, and your members to God as instruments for righteousness. For sin will have no dominion over you, since you are not under law but under grace.

What then? Are we to sin because we are not under law but under grace? By no means!

ROMANS 6:10–15 ESV

Before we become discouraged at our own lack of desire to do this, let's remember that we as believers in Christ are no longer in charge of our lives. We already know that we cannot put sin aside on our own. And just as we could not live perfectly apart from Christ, we cannot live the Christian life under our own steam, conquering sin under our own power. The Spirit must guide us into the Christian lifestyle that will please our Lord. As He empowers us, we will be able to live as He wants us to live.

So I say, let the Holy Spirit guide your lives. Then you won't be doing what your sinful nature craves. The sinful nature wants to do evil, which is just the opposite of what the Spirit wants. And the Spirit gives us desires that are the opposite of what the sinful nature desires. These two forces are constantly fighting each other, so you are not free to carry out your good intentions.

Galatians 5:16–17 NLT

But the fruit of the Spirit is love, joy, peace, forbearance, kindness, goodness, faithfulness, gentleness and self-control. Against such things there is no law. Those who belong to Christ Jesus have crucified the flesh with its passions and desires. Since we live by the Spirit, let us keep in step with the Spirit. Let us not become conceited, provoking and envying each other.

Galatians 5:22–26 NIV

This does not mean that God does all the work and we lie back lazily, expecting only good things to happen in our lives. We must make efforts to resist sin on a daily basis (see James 4:7). We need to walk in the Lord whom we have accepted:

This is the message we have heard from him and proclaim to you, that God is light, and in him is no darkness at all. If we say we have fellowship with him while we walk in darkness, we lie and do not practice the truth. But if we walk in the light, as he is in the light, we have fellowship with one another, and the blood of Jesus his Son cleanses us from all sin. If we say we have no sin, we deceive ourselves, and the truth is not in us.

1 John 1:5–8 ESV

The Christian life is demonstrated by the faithful works of the believer. Though works cannot get us into heaven, they are the result of our knowledge of our final destination and a measure of our willingness to please our Lord.

For we are God's masterpiece. He has created us anew in Christ Jesus, so we can do the good things he planned for us long ago.

Ephesians 2:10 NLT

Let your light so shine before men, that they may see your good works, and glorify your Father which is in heaven.

Matthew 5:16 KJV

"A good man brings good things out of the good stored up in him, and an evil man brings evil things out of the evil stored up in him."

MATTHEW 12:35 NIV

Good works and faith cannot be separated, because it takes trust in God to be able to do works that are really good.

Faith and obedience are bound up in the same bundle. He that obeys God trusts God; and he that trusts God obeys God. He that is without faith is without works; and he that is without works is without faith.

CHARLES H. SPURGEON

Works or deeds that we think are good but that we do under our own power cannot gain us heaven or God's approval. But with His Spirit working in us, we can both do good works and please our Lord.

This is the life God has in mind for His people.

CHAPTER 7
Living in Salvation

For, "Everyone who calls on the name of the Lord will be saved."
ROMANS 10:13 NIV

Except for its first word, Romans 10:13 is actually part of a passage in the Old Testament. Paul was quoting the prophet Joel's description of what would happen following a terrible Day of the Lord. This was a judgment day for God's people that would also include the blessing of salvation for some—those who would call on His name.

Today we are not certain when Joel lived and prophesied, so we cannot know the identity of the "great and powerful people" who caused the devastating day for those who believed in the Lord (see Joel 2:2 ESV). As this overpowering enemy attacked, God called His people to repentance, and the priests prayed that God would spare His people (see vv. 12–14, 17). He mercifully did. Then He promised to drive the enemy away and bless His people with many good things (see vv. 20–25). In verse 27 the prophet added the promise, "You shall know that I am in the midst of Israel, and that I am the Lord your God and there is none else. And my people shall never again be put to shame" (ESV).

As if the joy of that kind of intimate, protective relationship with God was not enough, the Lord continued through the prophet Joel:

> *"Then, after doing all those things, I will pour out my Spirit upon all people. Your sons and daughters will prophesy. Your old men will dream dreams, and your young men will see visions. In those days I will pour out my Spirit even on servants—men and women alike. And I will cause wonders in the heavens and on the earth—blood and fire and columns of smoke. The sun will become dark, and the moon will turn blood red before that great and terrible day of the Lord arrives. But everyone who calls on the name of the Lord will be saved, for some on Mount Zion in Jerusalem will escape, just as the Lord has said. These will be among the survivors whom the Lord has called."*
>
> Joel 2:28–32 NLT

Calling on God

Whether it was in Joel's day or today, the Lord promises to save those who call on Him. But what does it mean to call on God?

The first human to call on God was Abram, or Abraham, who "called upon the name of the LORD" (Genesis 12:8 KJV) after God appeared to him and promised to give him the land of Canaan. Abram had just entered this new land, after traveling many miles at God's command. What was he doing when he called on God? He was worshipping the Lord. Abram was thankful that he and his family had arrived safely, and he trusted that God would provide this land to them, too, though it was already inhabited by other people.

After being saved from King Saul's attempts on his life, King David praised the Lord, saying: "I will call on the LORD, who is worthy to be praised: so shall I be saved from mine enemies" (2 Samuel 22:4 KJV). David had repeatedly called on God for help as he fought against jealous King Saul, and God had kept him safe through many battles and other dangers. David knew the Lord who was faithful would aid him repeatedly.

When the prophet Elijah ended up in a face-off with the priests of the pagan god Baal, he proposed to the pagan priests:

And call ye on the name of your gods, and I will call on the name of the Lord: and the God that answereth by fire, let him be God. And all the people answered and said, It is well spoken.

1 Kings 18:24 KJV

Both sides in this spiritual conflict would worship their respective deities. The one who responded to their worship with fire would be the God whom all Israel should worship.

In the Psalms, God promises: "The Lord is near to all who call on him, to all who call on him in truth" (Psalm 145:18 ESV). He encourages us to worship Him.

What is the name of God that believers are calling on? "In biblical times," says *The Revell Bible Dictionary*, "names were more than mere labels. . . . The 'name of the Lord' is exalted because in his name God himself is suddenly present with the hearer, revealing both truth and his very self." So when believers call on God's name, they are doing more than simply calling Him "Jesus"—they are appealing to His authority and power.

In both the passage in Joel and in Romans, when God says that everyone who calls on Him will be saved, He's talking about those who believe in Him and worship Him as a regular part of their lives. His promise of salvation isn't some kind of blanket statement that covers the whole world—He didn't say "everyone will be saved." God is describing salvation that affects His people, the ones He has called into His kingdom.

Those Who Never Call

So what happens to those who never worship God? In His mercy, God saves some people, but not all of them. Just as Christians run into people who refuse to believe God and even become antagonistic toward Him, if He allowed everyone into heaven, eternity would constantly be trying to assimilate those who hated Him. Anyone who resists Him on earth would also resist Him in heaven. That wouldn't make it heaven for anyone—especially the ones who did not want to believe in Him and hated being in an environment that constantly glorified God.

Therefore God's justice punishes those who resist the sacrifice of the Son who died for their sins. They turned down the only opportunity for salvation, and He has allowed them to do that. God cannot ignore the rejection of the costly death of His Son.

If a child saw that another child was about to be hit by a car and ran to rescue that friend, being killed as he saved her, we would expect that rescued child and the parents to be extremely thankful. But what if the rescued child and her parents ignored the sacrifice or even criticized the family whose child died? We would feel the injustice deeply and would think the family of the child who died extremely naive if they just ignored the insult. Many people might confront the family of the rescued child about their heartlessness.

It's the same with Jesus' sacrifice. God gave Him to rescue the modern-day Adam, but if Adam ignores that rescue and defies the One who died for him, he has done a huge wrong to God. The Father cannot ignore that without doing an injustice to both the Son and Himself. So He allows the people who choose not to believe in Jesus to have their way and to end up in the torments of hell (see Matthew 16:23; Luke 16:23).

This is not to say that God rejoices in such punishment. "Do I take any pleasure in the death of the wicked? declares the Sovereign LORD. Rather, am I not pleased when they turn from their ways and live?" (Ezekiel 18:23 NIV). Nor should Christians stand by and rejoice at those who do not accept salvation. God has told them to reach out to the world (see Matthew 28:19–20), and they have done that, often taking risks to do so and putting up with negative reactions from the ones to whom they witness. But neither God nor those who follow the Lord can drag unbelievers, kicking and screaming, into heaven.

The Human Reaction

Many people feel dissatisfied with this heavenly sense of justice. They demand that God should save everyone or they will not believe in Him. They would like to have a god who asks little of them and accepts everyone blindly. But God is not blind or weak, and He will not take those who wish to come to Him only on their own terms. He is God, and He gets to call the shots. No person has the right to demand that God act as he expects Him to act. He is God and we are not.

Yet this does not mean that God is uncaring. Scripture tells us that He calls all people to come to Him. "God is faithful, who has called you into fellowship with his Son, Jesus Christ our Lord" (1 Corinthians 1:9 NIV). The truth is that if we were left to our own desires, caught in our own sin, we would never come to Him at all. The idea of worshipping God would never appeal to us, and we would never even think of it on our own. So God places Himself in the path of unbelievers and calls on them to trust in Him. His Spirit gently speaks to their hurting hearts so they will begin to have an understanding of His grace.

To work good in our lives, before we even had a spiritual thought, God reached out and called mankind to become part of His kingdom. Not all would come—yet He had already chosen that some would respond to His grace. Those would be glorified with Him in eternity.

And we know that in all things God works for the good of those who love him, who have been called according to his purpose. For those God foreknew he also predestined to be conformed to the image of his Son, that he might be the firstborn among many brothers and sisters. And those he predestined, he also called; those he called, he also justified; those he justified, he also glorified.

ROMANS 8:28–30 NIV

For he chose us in him before the creation of the world to be holy and blameless in his sight. In love he predestined us for adoption to sonship through Jesus Christ, in accordance with his pleasure and will—to the praise of his glorious grace, which he has freely given us in the One he loves. In him we have redemption through his blood, the forgiveness of sins, in accordance with the riches of God's grace that he lavished on us. With all wisdom and understanding, he made known to us the mystery of his will according to his good pleasure, which he purposed in Christ, to be put into effect when the times reach their fulfillment—to bring unity to all things in heaven and on earth under Christ.

EPHESIANS 1:4–10 NIV

We may not be able to understand why God did not simply say, "Everyone will be saved," but we can know that He had a purpose in doing this. The Lord does not do anything frivolously. Nor is this the first time God tells of saving only some people. In the Old Testament, whenever faith seemed ready to die and the situation appeared hopeless, God saved a remnant of people to glorify Him (see 1 Kings 19:18; 2 Kings 19:30–31; 2 Chronicles 36:20; Ezra 9:8).

The Results of Salvation

So what happens to our modern-day Adam who listens to the gospel message and calls on God's name?

Following the new map of salvation, he will experience God's plan for every believer on earth and will enter heaven when his life on earth ends. Along the way, he will have a better life. No longer will he spend his life trying to figure out how to get out of the ditch he was once stuck in. Though he will surely face the challenges of this life, these problems will not destroy him, as he seeks his Lord's counsel and follows His road. God's blessings will begin to touch him in this life and will be stored up for eternity.

In accepting Christ's salvation, Adam will have experienced what the apostle James describes: "He who turns a sinner from the error of his way will save a soul from death and cover a multitude of sins" (James 5:20 NKJV). The death-dealing sin he once lived in will no longer lay claim to his life, and he will experience the truth that Jesus' blood, offered on the cross, has covered his sins. Though he won't live a perfect Christian life, because no human is perfect, God will continually work in his life, and he will begin to look more and more like Jesus.

> *The Savior will sanctify His people, renew them, give them a hatred of sin, and a love of holiness. The grace that does not make a man better than others is a worthless counterfeit. Christ saves His people, not IN their sins, but FROM their sins. Without holiness, no man shall see the Lord.*
>
> Charles Haddon Spurgeon

Adam should immediately feel a change in his life. His spirit will connect with the Holy Spirit. He will know that he is no longer alone, that he has a powerful connection with his Savior, the Lord Jesus. Those sinful things that once appealed to Adam will no longer be so important, and many of these will soon become distasteful, while the things of God will become the focus of his life.

> *If thy heart be renewed, if thou shalt hate the things that thou didst once love, and love the*

things that thou didst once hate; if thou hast really repented; if there be a thorough change of mind in thee; if thou be born again, then hast thou reason to rejoice: but if there be no vital change, no inward godliness; if there be no love to God, no prayer, no work of the Holy Spirit, then thy saying "I am saved" is but thine own assertion, and it may delude, but it will not deliver thee.

Charles Haddon Spurgeon

Instead of rebelling against God and rejoicing in sin, if Adam seeks God daily, he will be increasingly eager to obey the Lord. Not because he wants to follow a lot of rules, but because He loves God, he will want to know Him more deeply and serve Him faithfully. By this other people will know the change of rebirth has occurred in his life. If this does not happen, there will be room to question whether he made a real commitment.

Obedience and the new birth go hand in hand: "For it is not those who hear the law who are righteous in God's sight, but it is those who obey the law who will be declared righteous" (Romans 2:13 NIV).

As our modern Adam recognizes all that his heavenly Father has done for him and increasingly desires to do the will of God, he will draw closer to his Lord by meeting with other Christians at church and in Bible study. More than that, when sin does tempt him and he fails to resist, he will hate the wrong that he has done and feel the separation it brings between him and Jesus. Pained by his own wrongdoing, Adam will seek to make things right again by confessing his sin to God and seeking His forgiveness. And he will feel the work of the Spirit in his heart, as he is again made clean by the blood of Christ.

No believer is completely without sin, as anyone who watches Christians for a while will discover. But the sin that continues to confront believers does not prove that they cannot live the Christian life. Instead, if they will not despair, it pushes them closer to Him. They recognize that their own concept of sinlessness is inadequate, and they begin to understand how deeply they need the salvation they have experienced in Jesus.

To mistake freedom from sin only on the conscious level of our lives for complete deliverance from sin by the atonement through the cross of Christ is a great error. No one fully knows what sin is until he is born again. Sin is what Jesus Christ faced at Calvary. The evidence that I have been delivered from sin is that I know the real nature of sin in me. For a person to really know what sin is requires the full work and deep touch of the atonement of Jesus Christ, that is, the imparting of His absolute perfection.

The Holy Spirit applies or administers the work of the atonement to us in the deep unconscious realm as well as in the conscious realm. And it is not until we truly perceive the unrivaled power of the Spirit in us that we understand the meaning of 1 John 1:7 [NKJV], which says, ". . .the blood of Jesus Christ His Son cleanses us from all sin." This verse does not refer only to conscious sin, but also to the tremendously profound understanding of sin which only the Holy Spirit in me can accomplish.

I must "walk in the light as He is in the light. . ."—not in the light of my own conscience, but in God's light. If I will walk there, with nothing held back or hidden, then this amazing truth is revealed to me: ". . .the blood of Jesus Christ His Son cleanses [me] from all sin" so that God Almighty can see nothing to rebuke in me. On the conscious level it produces a keen, sorrowful knowledge of what sin really is. The love of God working in me causes me to hate, with the Holy Spirit's hatred for sin, anything that is not in keeping with God's holiness. To "walk in the light" means that everything

> *that is of the darkness actually drives me closer to the center of the light.*
>
> OSWALD CHAMBERS

Amazingly, Adam will find that even when he does sin, God has provided him with a solution. Instead of pouring wrath down on him, the Spirit will continually call him to repentance, to turn again to Jesus, whose onetime sacrifice is effective even for sins committed by those who already know Him. All a believer who has fallen into sin needs to do is admit that he has again lost the way, ask for forgiveness, and focus on ending that sin in his life. That one who has erred will find:

> *He hideth our unrighteousness with His righteousness, He covereth our disobedience with His obedience, He shadoweth our death with His death, that the wrath of God cannot find us.*
>
> HENRY SMITH

As often as Adam returns to Jesus, confessing his own inability to end sin under his own power but wanting to do so, He will experience forgiveness. The cross will always be Adam's hope in his efforts to escape sin. As John Owen testified, "There is no death of sin without the death of Christ." Even the experienced Christian cannot fight sin alone. God alone ends sin, and even humanity's best efforts to fend it off will not work.

As Martin Luther discovered, Christians can only be justified with God through faith. That faith does not end when a person becomes a Christian. Instead, the Christian walk that follows will challenge Adam every day of his life as he learns more about his own inability to live faithfully under his own power and God's ability to fill him with His Spirit (see Romans 15:13; Ephesians 5:18; Colossians 1:9). Empowered to live faithfully, Adam will increasingly live in a way that glorifies God and demonstrates his own faith in Him. But Adam will never come to a point where he can overcome sin successfully in his own strength.

If he is wise, Adam will cultivate an obedient Christian life. Not only will he avoid and resist sin in his day-by-day experience, he will seek to take action and do good things:

> *Sin is to be overcome, not so much by direct opposition to it as by cultivating opposite principles. Would you kill the weeds in your garden, plant it with good seed; if the ground be well occupied there will be less need of the hoe.*
>
> ABRAHAM FULLER

By engaging in such a lifestyle, Adam will draw closer and closer to His Lord, appreciating Him and the eternal promises He offers. On earth Adam will experience the beginnings of eternal life and look forward to being with God in the afterlife. At times he will long to be with God in eternity. In 2 Corinthians 5:6–9 (ESV), the apostle Paul expressed this dichotomy between our earthly existence and God's heavenly promise:

> *We know that while we are at home in the body we are away from the Lord, for we walk by faith, not by sight. Yes, we are of good courage, and we would rather be away from the body and at home with the Lord. So whether we are at home or away, we make it our aim to please him.*

On earth, obedience to the Lord is a matter of faith. As Adam grows in his love of God, he will naturally increase in his desire to be with Him. God has prepared an eternity that Adam will long to share with Him. But as long as the faithful Adam remains on earth, he will obey and love the Lord more, looking forward to the eternal promise.

The Romans Road guides Christians to an intimate relationship with God. This leads us to recognize God's deep love working in our lives and to seek to appreciate all He has done for us. Martin Luther was grateful for the ability of the book of Romans to lead people into this kind of relationship:

> *This letter [the book of Romans] is truly the most important piece in the New Testament. It is purest Gospel. It is well worth a Christian's while not only to memorize it word for word but also to occupy himself with it daily, as though it were the daily bread of the soul. It is impossible to read or to meditate on this letter too much or too well.*

It would be wise for all Christians to take the Reformer's words to heart and study the book of Romans and other scriptures very carefully. Through scripture, we come to know our Lord—who He is, what He commands, and how we can best serve Him. This is the goal of the Romans Road while we are here on earth. And when we leave this life, we will join Jesus in eternity and forever celebrate the One whom we have known in this life.

When Adam gets to eternity, the destination will be more than he could have imagined as he traveled through the snowstorms and rainstorms of life on earth. And if he lives as a wise Christian, he will get to eternity with the things that really matter. By sending his treasures to heaven instead of hoarding things on earth, he will come into an inheritance of the heart (see Matthew 6:19–21). All those things he could not cram into his earthly truck will be useless in heaven, but the good deeds he did on earth will fill the coffers of heaven.

By continuing to grow in Christ, Adam and others who walk the Romans Road will discover that love for God continues to grow, until, like one of the Puritans, we can pray:

> *The more I love Thee with a truly gracious*
> *love the more I desire to love Thee, and the*
> *more miserable I am at my want of love;*
> *The more I hunger and thirst after Thee,*
> *the more I faint and fail in finding Thee,*
> *The more my heart is broken for sin,*
> *the more I pray it may be far more broken.*
>
> *My great evil is that I do not remember the*
> *sins of my youth, nay, the sins of one day I*
> *forget the next.*
> *Keep me from all things that turn to unbelief*
> *or lack of felt union with Christ.*
>
> THE VALLEY OF VISION

Our union with Christ is the goal of our Christian walk. May we draw nearer to Him with every passing day.

Scripture Index